AN AMERICAN ISLAND IN HITLER'S REICH

The Bad Nauheim Internment

AN AMERICAN ISLAND IN HITLER'S REICH

The Bad Nauheim Internment

Charles B. Burdick

School of Social Sciences
San Jose State University
San Jose, California

MARKGRAF
PUBLICATIONS GROUP
PO BOX 936
MENLO PARK, CA

Markgraf Publications Group
A division of The Robots Inc.
P.O. Box 936
Menlo Park, CA 94025

Printed and bound in the United States of America

ISBN 0-944109-00-4 PAPERBACK
0-944109-01-2 HARDCOVER
LIBRARY OF CONGRESS CATALOG CARD NUMBER 87-62229

FOR
DRUCILLA REDWINE, MAYNARD ROBINSON
AND
GEORGE SICULAR

The author, Charles B. Burdick, is Dean of the School of Social Sciences at San Jose State University, San Jose, CA. Dean Burdick holds an AB from San Jose State College, and MA and PhD degrees in History from Standford University. The former Fulbright-Hays scholar has received numerous awards for scholarship and is the only two-time awardee of the Outstanding Teacher Award, California State University and Colleges System.

Published works include the following books:

INSTITUTIONS OF THE GERMAN REVOLUTION, 1918–1919. New York: Praeger, 1965
GERMANY'S MILITARY STRATEGY AND SPAIN IN WORLD WAR II. Syracuse: Syracuse University Press, 1968
FURCHTLOS UND TREU; DAS LEBEN DES GENERAL HUBERT LANZ. Cologne: Markus Verlag, 1971
UNTERNEHMEN SONNENBLUME; DER ENTSCHLUSS ZUM AFRIKA-FELDZUG. Neckargemuend: Kurt Vowincki, 1972
RALPH LUTZ AND THE HOOVER INSTITUTION. Stanford: Hoover Institution Press, 1974
THE JAPANESE SIEGE OF TSINGTAU: WORLD WAR I IN ASIA. Hamden: Archon Press, 1976
THE FRUSTRATED RAIDER. Carbondale: Southern Illinios University Press, 1979
WORLD WAR II GERMAN MILITARY STUDIES.* New York: Garland, 1979, 28 volumes.
WASHINGTON SQUARE, 1857–1979. THE HISTORY OF SAN JOSE STATE UNIVERSITY.** San Jose: San Jose State University, 1980
WAR IN ASIA AND THE PACIFIC, 1939–1949.* New York: Garland, 1980. 13 volumes.
THE STORY OF THE GERMAN PRISONER AT BANDO, 1915–1920.** Tokyo: Orion, 1982 (in Japanese)
CONTEMPORARY GERMANY.* Boulder: Westview, 1984
THE GERMAN PRISONERS-OF-WAR IN JAPAN, 1914–1920. Washington, D.C.: University Press, 1984
THE LIFE OF GENERAL DER GEBIRGSTRUPPE HUBERT LANZ. Osnabruck: Biblio Verlag, 1986

*Co-editor
**Co-author

ACKNOWLEDGEMENTS

Any study of recent history rests on the existing documents (which are often fragmentary) and the surviving participants. The mixture of these sources is vital to accuracy and understanding. While the paper records are available for scholarly use, the gift of time and consideration from the surviving individuals is a precious one. I am indebted to everyone listed in the bibliography for assistance, I must list certain individuals who were supportive beyond words. In particular I confess my debt to Vice-Admiral Onnie Lattu. His insistance, his letters, his enthusiasm provided the motive force for the task.

In addition several other participants shared their time and thoughts in careful detail. Do let me thank Ernest Fischer, Captain Arthur Graubart, Stewart Herman, Jr., Dagfin Hoynes, Werner John, George Kennan, Norma Lovell, Frances Nordbye, Angus MacLean Thuermer for their numerous letters, thoughts, and assistance.

Clearly several individuals, not associated with the internment, provided aid. Here I am deeply obligated to Dr. Carl Boyd, Dr. Maria Keipert, Dr. David Mayers, Agnes Peterson and William Reckmeyer. Henry White Jr. provided information and allowed me to use excerpts from his father's poetry. They all provided much support.

The struggle to put everything together requires a group of understanding, patient, talented individuals who provide the realistic needs for progress. My debt to Leslie Brand, Lynn Cole, Nancy McAdams, and Emi Nobuhiro is truly large. They provided assistance beyond description.

At the end my enduring gratitude goes to two people. Maynard Robinson proved that one can return to academic endeavors despite administative responsibilities. Linda Garcia typed and suffered my handwriting; she is special—most, most special for her consideration and help.

The theme is narrow, the experience a moment in time, the historical value personal. Yet history is composed of individual stories. My gratitude to all who helped the research is overwhelming; my responsibility for any errors, sadly, manifest and clear.

Waiting . . .

CONTENTS

Acknowledgements i

Chapter I: Prelude to Internment 1

Chapter II: The Newsmen 17

Chapter III: Kennan Takes Charge 31

Chapter IV: Passing Time 59

Chapter V: Going Home 95

Bibliography 115

Berlin, Unter den Linden
facing Brandenburger Tor

CHAPTER I

PRELUDE TO INTERNMENT

The Winter slowly crawls across the land
Grey freezing mists enshroud the willing hills
Enforced presence numbs my limbs and thoughts,
And slower yet rolls on the undetermined time
of my deliverance.

Internment[1]

By December, 1941, Berlin, the former city of light and frivolity, had fallen on difficult times. Earlier one of the most exciting metropolises in all Europe, it had metamorphosed into a drab, lifeless urban mass at war. All of the grand hostelries which had entertained the famous and infamous of the past survived on their reputations; the splendid restaurants discarded their gaiety in favor of immediate survival; the legendary cultural milieu with its spiritual vitality simply disappeared into darkness. With paint peeling off the exteriors, bomb-shattered windows covered with plywood, empty store shelves protected by undated promissary notes, every building reflected the sudden, dramatic change in the great city. Everywhere the uncertain grim faces of the citizenry revealed their fearful prophecy of the future.

All consumers goods were in short supply, rationed by circumstances if not by regulation. No repairs to buildings, equipment, vehicles, or any decaying object were possible. Barter had already replaced money as the basic form of exchange. The pleasantries of life were gone in favor of the war effort. Even alcohol, which made some of these difficulties bearable, was in limited supply and obtainable only on the black market. Many bars had attractive arrays of bottles filled with colored water, but purveyed only the rawest of spirits. Christmas, 1941, was the driest in German history. Berlin provided a bleak, somber, and depressing image for anyone fated to seek survival in its environs. The dizzy, downward spiral made the essentials of life: food, clothing, and shelter very dear for everyone not well connected in the party. By December, 1941, the war was clearly not progressing as well as the omnipresent mobile street loudspeakers proclaimed, in ever shriller terms.

At night the city turned into a foreboding, dead sea of darkness. Officials enforced the strict blackout regulations with a ferocious Teutonic efficiency which made compliance a cardinal rule of human behaviour. Anyone moving about the city in the pervasive blackness did so at considerable peril. Even the simplest stroll was an adventure in uncertainty. One needed some knowledge of the neighborhood before venturing out.

By day the bizarre efforts at camouflaging the city and its landmarks created a macabre sense of unreality. With phoney stage props, guy wires, and varnished canvas erected to confuse and detour enemy bombing attacks, the artists posed scenes of colorful intensity but counterfeit reality. Huge, newly constructed, concrete towers, ugly pedestals for the shining anti-aircraft guns, provided a sobering harbinger of the future. Uniforms were in profusion. The voluble Berliners were reduced to incendiary witticisms about their brown-shirted leaders. They were a hardy people able to cope with the vicissitudes of life although few underestimated the manifest decline in their fortunes. While maintaining their individual dignity, many believed that the world-both in a global as well as in a personal sense-was out of control.[2] The removal of the 1940 victory platforms in late 1941 confirmed their pessimism.

Among the numerous depressed people in Berlin were a few Americans. Most of them were official government representatives or journalists, but they included some adventuresome souls stranded in Germany by the war. The diplomats and military attaches had little choice about their post. While desperately overworked attending to their responsibilities for prisoners of war, property, nationals, etc. of various powers, they had no impact on the events of their time. Beyond the hurly-burly of their daily activities, they observed world events via newscasts and lines plotted on wall maps. They served in an understaffed legation in an unfriendly country under difficult circumstances. The purposeful insolence of Nazi officials toward them constantly reminded them of their isolation and difficult position within the confines of the Third Reich.

The newsmen stayed on because of their innate curiosity concerning the historical forces whirling around them, their personal fascination with the banal power of Nazi Germany, and their powerful emotional commitment to competition with each other. While the Nazis created a tenuous *esprit de corps* among the correspondents, it was a spirit of enforced cooperation against a common foe rather than one of genuine trust or belief. They were as depressed and angry as their diplomatic representatives, but their desire to experience the intensity of what they perceived as the coming explosion kept them as fascinated, even though often bored observers. Each one wanted to be the last departee who would turn out the light.

U.S. Embassy in Berlin
lunch-hour garden party

Relations between Hitler's Germany and the United States had fallen into disrepair much earlier, with formality covering over the real chasm between them. America's Ambassador, Hugh Wilson, had departed for home on November 16, 1938, leaving a charge d'affaires to conduct official activities.[3] The intentional insult did not alter the legation's role in protecting the interests of numerous belligerents. In June, 1941, the Embassy officials had supervised the closure of the surviving American consulates in Germany, the repatriation of their personnel, and the transfer of their responsibilities to Berlin, the last outpost in Germany flying the United States flag. The net result was a disproportionate increase in work, with a corresponding decline in staff. For those who remained at their posts, the extent of their administrative obligations created a freneticism which eliminated boredom without resolving the general frustration. Existing in the Third Reich was not easy for most Americans.

Few of them possessed much tolerance for their Hitlerian hosts. Confronting the official anti-Semetic program each day along with the obvious falsehoods and manipulations of the Nazi propaganda machine was difficult and distressing. The diplomats also had to cope with the continuously uncertain relationships with the bureaucratic forces essential to their work: overbearing officials, Gestapo thugs, party hacks, petty self-seekers. As a result, service in Berlin was challenging but seldom with any positive overtones.

Francis Cunningham, Leland Morris, E. Tomlin Bailey, Lloyd Yates

The key people in the Embassy were Leland Morris, the Charge d'Affaires, and George Kennan, the First Secretary. They made an interesting pair. Morris, fifty-five years old, had joined the foreign service in 1910 and served in various positions, mostly in the Near and Middle East. Short, rotund, humorless, and slow-moving, he was by nature an administrator rather than a practicing diplomat.[4] His appointment, as an experienced consular officer was probably an intentional signal to the Germans (if not a calculated affront) that the Americans possessed little interest in genuine diplomatic intercourse with the Nazi regime.

Kennan, eighteen years his junior, had joined the foreign service in 1926 and served in the major European posts. He had earned a widespread reputation for his keen intellect, linguistic skill, and imperious manner. Tall, trim, and agile, he was an extrovert, but kept his distance and independence from others. He let a razor-sharp tongue, rather than any outward emotional display, explain his moods. In most social activities he was an observer as opposed to an active participant—standing apart, aloof, appraising with what appeared to be a slightly contemptuous smirk. Kennan was an extremely able diplomat, devoted to his trade, with analytical and organizational skills denied many of his contemporaries. Clearly he was a man on the rise.

Both men found their positions increasingly depressing and nerve-racking. The Germans had eliminated all social contact between their citizens and the Americans, controlled all non-official use of the telephone, and initiated the shadowing of Embassy personnel.[5] Also, Morris and Kennan had more than enough stress in making their responsibilities fit the available time. However, in a sense their frenetic work life was a blessing; their compatriots, the military attachés, fretted with precious little activity and less purpose.

The naval office had the more interesting people. Captain Adolph von S. Pickhardt, the attaché, was a tall figure of quiet dignity with a superb command of the German language. He was a man of good humor, but very conservative and set in his ways. A very private person, whenever possible he avoided the social scene leaving that activity to his younger associates. He was never afraid of decisions irrespective of the possible outcome; his associates found him a respected colleague, but not a potential friend.

Captain Adolph von S. Pickhardt
U.S. Naval Attaché, Berlin

His senior assistant attaché, and the senior sailor in terms of Berlin service, was Lieutenant Commander Arthur "Speedy" Graubart. A dedicated submariner, Graubart was sent by the Navy to Germany in 1931-1932 to learn something about the submersible engines they were purchasing from the Germans. He studied with Professor Hans Nagel in Dresden, obtaining an engineer's certificate. Clearly a free spirit, Graubart possessed an infectious joy in living and was the life of every party. He enjoyed good food, drink, and cigars, and he remained an endless raconteur of good stories. Besides his dedication to raising show dogs and playing enthusiastic tennis, he pursued his professional interests in technology with some diligence, but never overlooked a social event. He was clearly a man of the world.

Lt. Onnie P. Lattu
Commander A. H. Graubart

Lieutenant Commander Henry White had arrived in Berlin in February 1941. A large, burly man who had taken up flying in 1911 and possessed his certificate (#248) signed by Orville Wright, he was a fanatical flyer with little patience for non-aviators. White was a gifted musician (violin and guitar), knowledgeable linguist (with almost perfect mastery of seven languages), and a man of extensive factual knowledge. The Navy had recalled him to active service in 1941 and sent him immediately to Berlin.

The final assistant attaché was Lieutenant Onnie Lattu. He was a man of medium height, strong temperament, and physical drive. Unlike his associates, he loved the outdoors—hunting, fishing, hiking. Following an adventuresome trip—in which he had talked his way across the French, Swiss, and German frontiers without a visa—he had arrived in Berlin on September 17, 1940. He carried along two suitcases filled with cigarettes, coffee, and silk stockings. As a bachelor, he had his priorities in order.

The naval personnel found no opportunity for any work. After the fifty-destroyer arrangement between the United States and Great Britain, the Germans closed off all contacts and travel to them. The cumbersome restrictions also frustrated them through the difficult bureaucratic arrangements required for any meeting with Germans. As a result, they spent most of their time reading the German newspapers (more for comic relief than for information), chatting with equally frustrated attachés from other foreign countries, and drinking coffee. They were a bored group.

Capt. Adolph Pickhardt
Col. William Hohenthal

While burdened with many of the problems confronting their naval colleagues, the army attachés made some attempt at observing conditions in Berlin. They were a professional group seeking as much information as they could find, if only for future reference. The senior officer was Lieutenant Colonel William "Uncle Bill" Hohenthal, an avuncular, quiet man of intense dedication and wide experience. As the oldest man in the office, he perceived his Berlin service as a career, while his colleagues pursued theirs as an assignment. His colleagues envied his German language skills, his devotion, and his steady efficiency. Unlike many others, he never allowed his personal life to interfere with his professional concerns.

Lieutenant Colonel Harvey "Smitty" Smith was similiar to Hohenthal in personality, although more rotund in physique. A confirmed "tanker" officer, he seldom pursued interests in any other military area. While limited with the language, he enjoyed an insightful, sharp intellect which overcame much of his problem with German. Using his intuition and reflection, he obtained much respect for sound judgment and professional fairness.

The junior officer was Major Jack Lovell, perhaps the brightest of the entire attaché group. At West Point, from which he graduated in 1927, he had been a boxer, and he never lost this interest (he coached the 1936 Olympic boxing team). Subsequently he was detailed as an American student for the German General Staff School. Lacking any language skills, he started a summer course which terminated with the outbreak of war, stranding him in Berlin. He possessed a keen wit, learned quickly, and possessed an instinct for picking up facts in interesting places. Lovell carefully charted bomb hits in Berlin, assessed the damage, and made detailed evaluations of this information for future use.[7]

Despite their more strenuous endeavors, the soldiers really did not accomplish much. What little they collected and tabulated could not be sent home. Like their naval counterparts they often filled time with unexciting expedients. They did argue more about the issues of war, and they laid wagers as to when and how the Americans would join the conflict. Wolfinberger, taking the disputes seriously, prepared a long paper predicting war during the coming winter. He argued that President Roosevelt's tightening the flow of war materiel to Japan and sending supplies to Britain and Russia would change international power dynamics. At a given point circumstances would force Hitler to seek Japan's help. Given Wolfinberger's assumption that the Fuehrer would succeed in making this alliance, he proposed that Japan would attack both the United States and Great Britain in December 1941.[8]

Since the wives of the married attachés were back in the United States, most of the attaches joined in renting the former French Library at 25 Budapester Strasse, where they established a little America. With the advantages of the State Department Commissary, combined with those of being foreign diplomats (which allowed their purchase of Danish dairy products and German produce), they were a privileged class. They had a decent wine cellar and numerous servants, without overbearing responsibilities.

The building became a social center for many Americans and foreigners. They had a July 4 celebration, a Thanksgiving dinner, musicales, innumerable cocktail parties, and affairs for specific nationalities. While few Germans would risk party and police disfavor by attending, many foreign attachés and nationals enjoyed the American largess. One of the few Berliners willing to do so on a continuing basis was the old First World War sea raider, Captain Felix von Luckner. The attachés social events attracted much attention, not all of it friendly. When Graubart discovered a listening device in the chandelier, he carefully informed their guests that they always had at least one more visitor than those listed on the guest list. Thereafter many of them gathered near the "bug" and sang the praises of the Third Reich.[9]

In the harsh German winter they complained about the irony of their cozy living situation, contrasting with their isolation and uncertainty in a totalitarian community at war. This existence in a state of suspense came to an abrupt end during the evening of December 7, when Kennan picked up a short-wave report of the Japanese attack on Pearl Harbor. He immediately informed Morris, and they contacted as many of their colleagues as they could locate by telephone. They met later that night, seeking a plan of action, since war between the United States and Germany seemed certain.[10]

For the next few days uncertainty over a possible conflict reigned supreme, albeit everyone in the Embassy prepared for the anticipated declaration of war. The basic administrative requirements were already in place. In May, 1941, the Department of State had forwarded instructions to Morris for implementation, should diplomatic relations between the two powers be severed permanently. His orders specified that he should work out a transfer of American interests and responsibilities with the Swiss representatives, arrange for a local bank to liquidate the staff's financial affairs, terminate all alien employees, destroy confidential material, and maintain the repatriation rights for all American citizens. His instructions added the customary escape clause that the responsible authorities should "...feel free to use their judgment and common sense, and it [State Department] will support any reasonable action...even though such action is not expressly sanctioned by standing instructions...."[11]

On December 8 the Embassy employees followed these instructions. In contrast to the feverish efforts of the other offices, the Navy attachés office had little to do other than destroying their code books. In October Lattu and Graubart had asked Pickhardt if they should write a note requesting official permission to destroy office records. Pickhardt had replied that such action would require numerous conferences, and various messages and be a general waste of time. He had simply written out a brief note to the Navy Department, explaining that circumstances forced the destruction of everything except the code books. After its dispatch they had carefully executed his instructions.[12]

Lt. Lattu
Capt. Pickhardt

Everyone in the Embassy was busy with clearing out desks, burning all but the most necessary papers, and preparing for the inevitable conflict. Although no one received any official details, numerous friends in the Nazi party and diplomatic circles informed the Americans on December 9 that Hitler would be in Berlin on December 10 or 11 to declare war against the United States. In the course of the same day the Embassy telephones stopped functioning, and the Germans ceased accepting telegrams. Kennan and Morris agreed that this information was sufficient for final action. They ordered the destruction of everything, which kept all of the employees busy. The measure of their industry was a warning from a German building inspector that their fires were burning with excessive intensity and threatened adjacent buildings. Certainly the ashes of the burning papers drifted lazily over the neighborhood. They provided quiet reminders of the changed diplomatic relationships. Everyone participated, including Lattu, who had left for Stockholm on December 6, had dinner there, and flown back (against explicit orders) the following day. In addition to the long work details, the Americans sought contact with their German friends and colleagues for hasty goodbyes.

The next day the number of guards posted around the Embassy increased noticeably, and everyone who left the building acquired an escort. On December ll the large city square in front of the Embassy slowly filled with people. A loudspeaker truck appeared and parked directly in front of the building; a delicate, but obvious insult. Both Hitler's and Goering's automobiles passed through Pariser Platz en route to the Reichstag building for the Fuehrer's speech. The few Americans watching through the closed metal blinds fervently hoped that some of the soot from the burning documents fell on the Nazi leaders. Everyone listened to the radio, however, in order to capture the historic moment.

At 2:07 p.m. in answer to Goering's sycophantic plea, "Fuehrer, speak to us," Hitler began his address. He reviewed the progress of the war, the serious military difficulties in Russia, and the American desire for conflict. His references to Roosevelt and the latter's pursuit of capitalistic war were particularly savage. Following a long litany of historical complaints, Hitler called Roosevelt insane and announced that he had given the American Charge d' Affaires his passports. He closed by announcing the Italian-German-Japanese agreement for a war against the United States.[13]

The applause was thin and without force. Those in attendance clapped with thoughtful, uncommitted politeness. The harrangue clearly was not Hitler's best, and it reflected his fatigue and strain. Those Germans in front of the American Embassy quietly huddled in small groups, discussing the fateful announcement. They made no hostile gestures, showed no emotion. Inside the building the Americans had listened to the fateful announcemnt as well. The German propaganda ministry had stationed a radio truck outside the Embassy. Its high volume rocked the windows with Hitler's harsh tones. The Fuehrer had finally declared the World War.

As the Fuehrer began his speech the telephone in the American Embassy mysteriously came to life. Kennan answered and learned from an unidentified German official that a vehicle would arrive shortly to take Morris to the foreign office. The official appeared almost instantaneously and hurried Morris off on his mission. In route Morris' car ran afoul of a traffic policeman who refused passage into the Wilhelmstrasse. After a sharp exchange he proceeded but the delay did not help his mood. At the foreign office other functionaries ushered Morris into a long room with the German foreign minister, Joachim von Ribbentrop, and his translator, Paul Schmidt, who was present in case some phrase exceeded Morris' language skills. Ribbentrop advanced half way, bowed stiffly, kept Morris standing, and read the German note announcing a state of war. He added that repatriation of the Americans in Germany would be implemented immediately. Although von Ribbentrop spoke good English he read the German text as rapidly as he could. However, he stumbled over the name of the destroyer, *Reuben James* (calling it the "Robin James"). At the end he added in shrill tones, "...that President Roosevelt had consistently followed a policy aimed at war. Now he had got the war he desired." With that gratuitous remark he terminated the meeting, although he approved Morris' request for permission to cable the message to Washington, D.C. The entire exchange lasted just over three minutes.

Schmidt accompanied Morris to the door and quietly shook hands in departure. As Morris left, the German Chief of Protocol, Count Dornberg, came up, shook hands, and asked Morris to return that evening at 6:00 p.m. with Kennan.

They returned as instructed, and Morris gave Dornberg a note establishing the American view concerning the treatment and repatriation of the diplomatic representatives. It also included some remarks on the same issues for the German group in the United States. Dornberg seemingly had not reflected carefully on this latter issue and indicated, in some confusion, that he could not comment on the potential disposition of the Americans until he had more details concerning the status of the German diplomats. He would inform them about these plans in good time. Until he had more details, the Americans were free to move about the city.[16]

Harry A. Francis
Embassy radio operator

On Friday, December 12, the expectant Americans remained in their empty offices, waiting for some word concerning their immediate fate. Morris kept everyone in the building, despite much grumbling about the wasted time and lack of direction. Graubart and Lovell, bored with the inactivity, turned to the three empty safes belonging to the attachés office. They opened the two smaller ones and attached slips detailing the combinations. Perversely, they put their collectively owned formal top hat, despised by both men, in the larger safe and locked it. They wished the Nazis the worst.[17] After the Nazi foreign office reported that they would not be making any decisions that day, Morris let everyone depart at 7:00 p.m. He gave out careful instructions that everyone should avoid unpleasantries with the local populace, not speak English in public places, and report back to the Embassy the following morning.

The next day the German Foreign Office finally established a meeting with Kennan and Morris for 11:00 a.m. Dornberg informed them that they would be leaving the following day, about noon. He refused any clarification concerning their eventual destination. They would be "somewhere else in Germany." The Americans could take whatever baggage they wanted without limit, but they must be in the American Embassy by 10:00 a.m. Since the meeting was their last with von Dornberg, the latter asked Kennan to return that evening to meet the German official assigned to the group.

On their return to the Embassy, Morris and Kennan discussed the issue briefly, reached accord, informed their fellow diplomats of the development, and provided directions for everyone. Since the following day, December 14, was a Sunday and therefore Berlin would have very few taxis, they ordered that all baggage be in the Embassy that night. Tardy excuses would not be accepted. With these instructions came the designation of five monitors and the names of their group members. The former were responsible for the timely delivery of baggage and the appearance of their charges the following morning. The instructions suggested that the Americans would probably be interned for two weeks, and that each person should have 200 Reichsmarks. Obviously, the news despite the short time line, heralded a promptitude of action.

While everyone hurriedly completed his or her packings, Kennan returned to the foreign office where he met Legationssekretaer and SS Hauptsturmfuehrer (Captain) Valentin Patzak. An extremely tall (6'5"), handsomely built man of almost forty years, he had experienced the historical vicissitudes of his peer group. Forced out of school by his parental business misfortunes, Patzak had worked as a construction laborer, a salesman, and as a business representative for an American firm. Concurrently, he joined the Nazi Party and the SA in 1931. With the support of the party, he resumed his studies while working with Nazi student groups. He completed his studies in 1938, joined the SS, and became the student leader of the Berlin University.

SS Hauptsturmfuehrer (Captain)
Valentin Patzak, and wife

Kennan recognized immediately that Patzak would be a useful man and evaluated the Nazi with care. Patzak enjoyed limitless energy, good intelligence, and a strong will. He judged matters quickly, reached decisions with equal dispatch, and assured implementation. While formal and reserved by nature, he was punctiliously correct but never mean or tactless. He was certain of his own responsibilities, however, and would fulfill them properly and precisely—no matter what the local American or German officials might not like. Patzak as a superior adminstrator implemented decisions quickly and carefully. He had total authority but did not misuse it.

Patzak and Kennan worked until 10:00 p.m., organizing the sleeping car assignments in the three first- and second-class cars and the three third-class cars. The status and category of all the individuals required evaluative consideration, and became even more complicated when Patzak informed Kennan that the American journalists in Berlin would be included in the party. While considering the ranking Embassy personnel, they placed the senior newsmen and as many women as possible in the better accommodations.

While Patzak and Kennan worked the Americans brought in an ever-expanding mountain of baggage and personal effects. Morris had discouraged people from bringing too much but he could not inspect everyone's baggage. The lack of time, absence of local storage facilities, and simple confusion precluded strong administrative action.[18] The obvious misuse of the freedom disturbed Morris's sense of reality. As he watched the people moving their household goods in the middle of a war he marvelled at the strangeness of human behavior.[19] People appeared with chests of drawers, full sets of china, candelabra, bird cages, lamps, etc. In sum, the scene was one akin to a disorganized flea market. The more practical individuals, a definite minority, purchased whatever they could from the Embassy stores and packed basic foodstuffs. Some, like "Speedy" Graubart, had read about the internments in the First World War and acted on that knowledge. He had three suitcases; one he filled with all the cigars he could find, one he filled with champagne, and one he used for clothes.

As everyone hurriedly completed his or her final efforts—which included selling or giving away any surplus clothing, presenting gifts to servants and friends, and exchanging addresses for post-war contact—Kennan, already overworked and tired, received a note from Herbert J. Burgman. The latter was a strange, nervous man who was the chief clerk in the attaché office, where he had worked since 1920. While he had been mainly responsible for economic reports, he had access to the office files, had knowledge of the attachés over a long period, and had long understanding of the official priorities within the office. Burgman requested a delay in reporting, for medical reasons and for resolving his wife's business interests in Germany. He could not leave with the group, he wrote. A furious Kennan demanded that Burgman participate with the others. But Burgman did not appear, and subsequently he defected to the Nazis.[21]

The group gathered the following morning in a light rain. Everyone was present well in advance of the deadline. A number of police, plainclothes men, and a scattering of soldiers, both in and outside the building, reminded everyone that they were in an uncertain situation. A handful of individuals concluded their final responsibilities: turning in vehicles, clearing the Embassy stores area and account books, making the final tour of the building. Since no single room provided adequate space for the group, they divided into their travel groups without direction. Most of the departees enjoyed the first part of their waiting period, listening to the tales of the American journalists who had just joined the party that morning. The correspondents did have an adventurous story.

NOTES

[1]The leitmotifs come from poems written by Lieutenant Commander Henry J. White during the internment. I am indebted to Henry J. White, Jr. for them.

[2]There are few descriptions of life in 1941 Berlin. Useful accounts include Howard K. Smith, *Last Train from Berlin* (New York: Alfred Knopf, 1942), p 128f; Arvid Friedborg, *Behind the Steel Wall; a Swedish Journalist in Berlin, 1941-1943* (New York: Viking Press, 1944), p 56f; George F. Kennan, *Memoirs, 1925-1950 (Boston: Little Brown, 1964),* p. 107f. The best single account, although the author had departed by December, remains William L. Shirer, *Berlin Diary. The Journal of a Foreign Correspondent, 1934-1941* (New York: Alfred Knopf, 1941). The same author's *20th Century Journey; a Memoir of a Life and the Times* Vol II, *The Nightmare Years, 1930-1940* (Boston: Little Brown, 1984) is less helpful. Harry W. Flannery, *Assignment to Berlin* (New York: Alfred Knopf, 1942) provides some insights.

[3]There are numerous general accounts focusing on relations between the two countries albeit the subject requires a new, thoughtful study. Gerhard Weinberg's "Hitler's Image of the United States," *American Historical Review* 69 (July, 1964): 1006-21 provides interesting reading. Saul Friedlander, *Prelude to Downfall: Hitler and the United States, 1939-1941* (New York: Alfred Knopf, 1967 is of some value. The most recent general study is Manfred Jonas. *The United States and Germany, a Diplomatic History* (Ithaca: Cornell University, 1984).

[4]Morris had been interned by the Turks in the First World War. Stationed in Istanbul when relations were broken, he and some two dozen of his colleagues were put on a guarded train, the windows painted black, and provided food for two days. Because of some fighting they required five days travel to Vienna.

When they arrived in Vienna, they found no welcoming guards and asked the only uniformed figure on the platform, the station master, what to do. He suggested that they enjoy a meal at a nearby hotel and return the following Tuesday for their train's departure. He added that the opera had a particularly good performance that night. Conversation with Dr. Robert Levenson, a nephew of Leland Morris, August 1979.

Some Embassy employees found Morris a gregorious, likeable colleague and enviable poker player until his family arrived in Berlin. Thereafter he became more pretentious and withdrawn. Interview, Dagfin Hoynes, October, 1985.

[5]Morris reported home the earlier remarks of a German official, "We will put spotters on the American Embassy as soon as the time comes." He added the quiet observation that the French Embassy in Berlin had noted the use of spotters about two months before the onset of the war. Morris to Secretary of State, 24 February, 1941. State Department File 124.62/251 and 124.62/252. In the same dispatch he included a copy of a report which concluded, "I have no objections to having my movements observed, but I think it is a reflection on my intelligence to have such dumb persons set on my trail that every move they make is obvious."

[6]This material stems from discussions with Captain Arthur Graubart, 27 April 1980; Vice Admiral Onnie Lattu, May 1981; correspondence with both men; letter from Henry J. White, Jr, July 1981; conversation with Mrs. Henry J. White, 1 April 1981; biographical materials made available by Dr. Dean Allard, Center for Naval History.

[7]These observations come from the interviews with Graubart and Lattu; letter from Angus McLean Thuermer, 14 August 1980; letter from Mrs. Harold Hennessy (earlier Hohenthal), 6 September 1980, letter from Mrs. Jack Lovell, 28 July 1980; letter from Gene Stadler, 21 August 1980; various biographical papers made available by Robert E. Schnare, Special Collections, US Military Academy.

Mrs. Lovell, en route with her three children and a pet, got entangled in the 1939 conflict as well. After long delays created by the German mobilization she reached Berlin where Embassy personnel put her and her family on a train for Copenhagen the following day. She remained there until she received a transit visa to Italy where she remained until June 1940.

[8]Talk by Onnie Lattu, 2 November 1942, copy furnished by Admiral Lattu.

[9]After the Second World War when Graubart headed the Office of Naval Intelligence in Germany (1946-1952) he had a visitor from the Federal Bureau of Investigation. The latter played a scratchy tape recording of Graubart and Lovell praising Hitler's contributions to world affairs. The federal agent suggested that his agency had no interests in explanations and would destroy the tape. At the same time he proposed that a man in Graubart's position should exercise more caution. Nothing more was said. Interview with Captain Graubart, 27 April 1980. One of the cleaning maids told Graubart that he and his friends should burn their waste, since the Gestapo required her to bring them the contents of all wastebaskets. An appreciative Graubart sent her packages after 1945 until her death. Ibid.

[10]Kennan, *Memoirs,* pp 134-135. They were much concerned about their fate. As custodians of British interests they had been involved with a group of British consular officers interned for eighteen months. They lacked any assurance of the traditional politeness normally associated with diplomacy. The Nazi thugs were not always concerned with niceties. George Kennan, "Draft of Internment Story," pp. 1-2, File "1942" in Box 25, Kennan Papers, Princeton University.

Likewise finding a neutral border for exchanging diplomats was not a simple task in 1941. Even the concept of safe conduct for all of the belligerents was uncertain. In an age of barbarism the rules' interpretations lent themselves to anecdotal administration.

[11]State Department to American Embassy, Berlin, 25 May, 1941. File 124.62/256A

[12]Interview with Graubart, who treasured the decision as one of the few decisive moments by a superior officer in his long naval career.

[13]Max Domarus, *Hitler - Reden und Proklamationen, 1932-1945, Vol II, Untergang, 1939 - 1945* (Munchen: Suddeutscher Verlag) (note II 1963)

[14]The rationale for what seems in retrospect a foolish mistake has created an interesting discussion among historians. The most recent effort is Gerhard L. Weinberg's useful paper, "Die deutsche Politik gegenuber den Vereinigten Staaten im Jahr 1941: in Jurgen Rohwer and Eberhard Jackel, eds, *Kriegswende. Dezember 1941* (Koblenz: Bernard & Graefe, 1984), pp. 73-79 and the useful discussion of his paper, *Ibid*, pp. 104-129. See also Gerhard L. Weinberg, *World in the Balance. Behind the Scenes of World War II* (Hanover, N. H.: University Press of New England, 1981), pp. 75-95; Eberhard Jackel, Die deutsche Kriegserklarung an die Vereinigten Staaten von 1941," in *Im Dienste Deutschlands und die Rechtes. Festschrift fur Wilhelm G. Grewe zum 70. Geburtstag am l6. October 1981* hrag. Friedrich J. Kronek and Thomas Oppermann (Baden-Baden: Nomas Verlag, 1981), pp. 117-137. A dated study useful in this context in Captain Tracy B. Kittridge, "A Military Danger. The Revelation of Secret Strategic Plans," *United States Naval Institute Proceedings,* 81 (July, 1955), pp. 731-743. One needs to review the interrogations of the Nazi diplomats and military leaders as well as the intelligence intercepts, which cast some light on the issue. Letter from Carl Boyd, Old Dominion University, 19.IX.84.

[15]The descriptions come from Kennan, *Memoirs,* p. 135; Paul Schmidt, *Statist auf Diplomatischer Buhne, 1923-1945. Erlebnisse des Chefdolmetschers im Auswartigen Amt mit den Staatsmannern Europas* (Wien: Ullstein Verlag, 1953), p. 552; United States, Department of State, *Documents on German Foreign Policy, 1918-1945* Series D Vol. 12 (Washington, D.C.: Government Printing Office, 1964) pp. 999-1000 (#572), p. 1004 (#577)

Morris remarked on von Ribbentrop's problems with the *Reuben James,* "I had a curious feeling that he had mixed the Reuben James with the Robin Moor, the merchant ship also torpedoed a short time earlier. The thought crossed my mind that the Germans had sunk so many boats they couldn't keep them straight." This story is in numerous newspaper accounts in Morris' personnel file. State Department Life 123 M 83/550.

[16]Morris to Secretary of State, 11 December, 1941, File 124.62/280. Dornberg suggested to the liberal American proposal; "This puts everything in a different light. You people can go back to your homes and go on living as you have been. You can work at closing up your office, but you can't do any diplomatic or consular business, and we can allow you only local telephone service, on a reduced scale. You can't make any long distance calls. We'll try to let you know definitely tomorrow what is going to become of you." Kennan, "Story," p. 7.

Kennan asserts that the repatriation issue then went to Hitler for decision, who proposed on l3 December, "By the end of the week the Americans must be out of Berlin." Kennan, *Memoirs,* p. 136.

[17]After the Second World War, a member of the new German intelligence service quietly informed Graubart, with a knowing wink, that the Nazi officials had cut a hole through the back of the safe with some difficulty and had then carefully, and methodically cut the hat into pieces, looking for a secret transmitter. Interview with Graubart.

[18]George F. Kennan, "Report, the Internment and Repatriation of the American Official Group in Germany - 1941-1942" (nd but received in Washington, D.C. June 27, 1942), pp 1-6. Cited hereafter as "Kennan Report." Kennan printed an abridged version with the same title in *The American Foreign Service Journal* (August, September, 1942) pp 422-446; 473-477; 502-507. Also Lt. Col. Harvey H. Smith and Major J. R. Lovell, "The Story of the Internment, December 14, 1941 - May 12, 1942" (mimeographed, April 20 [sic], 1942) Cited hereafter as "Story" This report was for an inner circle of the internees. Mrs. J. R. Lovell kindly provided a copy. Henry J. White, "Diary," 9-14 December 1941. Mr. Henry J. White, Jr, kindly made the diary available. Much of the information on Patzak comes from his "Parteistatische Erhebung 1939" provided by the Berlin Document Center; letter from Frau Elfriede Patzak, 8 October 1984. The phonetic pronunciation of Patzak's name, Pacheck, quickly fell prey to the journalistic version of Pay Check. Letter from Angus Maclean Thuermer, 9 October 1985.

[19]Information from Robert Levinson.

[20]Graubart interview.

[21]Burgman was obviously a man with psychological problems, who earned his position through good fortune at the beginning and remained through longevity. He was extremely nervous and frightened about any responsibility. His work was adequate, but he was never a full member of the attache team. Various attachés did not trust him and viewed him as a probable spy. At his subsequent trial the court psychologist certified him as paranoid schizophrenic. In 1942 Burgman helped create station "Debunk", an anti-American radio program. Employing the name "Joe Scanlon" he used the staccato style of Walter Winchell as his model. In addition to his broadcasting he wrote numerous scripts and supervised the recording of the material. He stood trial in Washington, D.C. where he received a sentence of 6 to 20 years. Letter from George Kennan, 22 January 1979; Interview with Mrs. Katherine Smith, 8 July 1983; interview with Major General Arthur Vanaman, June 1982. For a description of the general operation of Burgman's German activities see David G. Wittels, "Hitler's Short Wave Rumor Factory," *The Saturday Evening Post*, 215 (November 21, 1942) pp. 12-13, 117-118, 122-125; William L. Shirer, "The American Radio Traitors", *Harper's Magazine*, 187 (October 1943), pp. 377-404. The trial papers are in the District Court of the United States for the District of Columbia, Case #442-49. Clearly he suffered from what Goethe termed the "malignancy of littleness."

Dr. Baum
Lt. Onnie Lattu
Dr. Charles Spicknall

Major Wm. Wolfinbarger, U.S. Army

CHAPTER II

THE NEWSMEN

The honeyed word, the servile bow
Yield to the iron hand
Around the prison stone they sit
The journalistic band.
The Ballad of Nauheim Gaol

Being a newsman in Berlin was not a simple assignment. The reporters confronted a wide range of daunting problems not understood elsewhere by the practitioners of a free press. First of all, there were the trials of living in Berlin. While the diplomats suffered from isolation and uncertain purposes they enjoyed assured food and shelter. The journalists, on the other hand, were in a no-man's land where they competed with the German civilians for food and drink, basic amenities and, above all housing. In the eyes of most Germans they were unwanted spectators who could be counted on to file false reports to their countrymen at home. The Nazi bureaucracy wanted nothing to do with the journalists beyond speeding their departure.

Beyond personal survival, the newsmen had professional problems. Their major concern was to determine the authenticity of information; i.e., the authencity of their few sources and the confirmation of source information. There were numerous anti-Nazis in the German bureaucracy who provided material through telephone conversations, at social events, or via pre-arranged meetings. These often long and deeply held associations rested on a foundation of mutual trust. As the conflict progressed, however, Germans became more afraid and thus less accessible to foreign journalists. The Nazi police became more efficient with time despite their sometimes cumbersome controls and dubious intellectual reputation. As the sources dried up, the journalists found greater reasons not to endanger them. If his government source were apprehended or uncovered somehow, the journalist would lose his visa and leave the country for freedom, but his informant confronted a more serious fate of imprisonment and torture. As a result the journalists hoarded their few valued sources and traded information with each other carefully.

Confronted with a narrowing field of sources the newsmen also had to cope with the Nazi approach to censorship. The propaganda officials knew how to utilize self-censorship as a control mechanism. Rather than physically censoring every line in a newsman's dispatches, they passed some which subsequent review found unacceptable or damaging to the regime. The offending journalists suffered personal lectures for their offenses or simply received an order to leave Germany. In this fashion, any writer anxious for an immediate departure home had a constantly available device. Those who felt an obligation or interest to remain played a ferocious game akin to the moth dancing around the candle's flame. Obviously this tightrope of nerves occasioned a constant struggle between the active stress of involvement and the depressing concerns of the Berlin blues. With fewer and fewer German contacts, in sharp competition with one another, harrassed by the Nazi officials, the newsmen were in an impossible situation. The list of journalists forced out of Germany was a lengthy one (between 1933 and 1937 more than forty writers departed without replacement). Concealment, double-meaning, word selection, or obscure idioms provided various tricks which facilitated dispatches through the German censors. Nonetheless, the Faustian bargain between integrity and residence was omnipresent.

Glen Stadler

Ed Schanke, Pat Conger
Jean Graffis, Glen Stadler

Their lot grew more complicated after the June 1941 German attack on the Soviet Union. The Germans stopped inviting them to various press conferences, harried them with telephone calls at odd hours, insulted them and their government both in public and in direct personal confrontations, and made explicitly clear that Americans were undesirable guests. Finding life exasperatingly temporary, the journalists ceased all planning. Since they never knew when the Gestapo would bang on their door, they destroyed all notes immediately after use and kept no files. As the Germans' hostility shifted to such direct methods, the journalists reached common accord that Germany and the United States could not avoid conflict. Nonetheless they wagered that mid-1942 was the probable date for a declaration of war. They did not want to miss the excitement of being present for that historical moment.

As a result, the news of Pearl Harbor caught them totally by surprise. Several were out of town or busy with other needs. Since their rights were uncertain under these new circumstances, they quickly assumed a low profile with tenuous telephone links with each other for security purposes. Usually they called their offices once very hour.

Just before midnight on December 9, Ed Shanke, who had the night duty for the Associated Press Bureau called Louis Lochner, the chief of the office. He reported the news that the American authorities had arrested some German journalists in the United States. While neither man knew any details or the circumstances prompting the action, they were reasonably certain that the Germans would take reprisal action. Shanke, a younger reporter, known as an inventive prankster, was deadly serious this time. He was a long way from Milwaukee.

The next day several journalists sought information and guidance through the American Embassy and trusted German officials. One of the latter group unsettled the journalists, remarking that any reprisal action would be accomplished in "the noblest manner."

In the afternoon of December 10 several American newsmen attended the regularly scheduled press conference. The small groups of foreign journalists scattered around the hall reflected uncertainty about the new conditions. Various individuals quietly stopped for a foreboding farewell to the Americans. Clearly the news had spread through their small community and everyone assumed some prompt German counteraction. As the heavyset, highly ambitious Paul Schmidt, von Ribbentrop's press spokesman, entered the room, quiet settled on the group. Schmidt was not popular with the press because of his innate vanity and obsessive hatred of Roosevelt, nonetheless, he commanded attention through his influential position and fleshy bulk. Moving with a slight slouch, his head bent over his heavy neck, "Newspaper Schmidt" was always an aggressive, predatory figure. As soon as he noticed the Americans, he stopped moving and shouted "One moment, please! The German correspondents in the United States have, contrary to custom and a gentleman's agreement, been arrested by the American authorities. I must, therefore, ask the American correspondents here present to leave the room and proceed forthwith to their homes."

As the Americans started towards the door their colleagues, acting on impulse, formed an exit aisle, and shook hands with their departing colleagues. The act of solidarity even included the Japanese press representatives, who participated in the farewell. At the door the imperious Schmidt solemnly and silently shook hands with each American. Afterwards he informed the remaining press representatives that the Reich intended nothing personal in the action, that any subsequent undertaking would not embarrass anyone, and that, hence-forth, the American correspondents, "do not exist for you or us."[2]

Gordon Knox
(self-portrait)

The word "house arrest" spread quickly among the remaining American correspondents. Prepared by their experiences over the past months, they expected prompt internment. With this clear warning they began settling their outstanding accounts, saying goodbye to friends, packing a small suitcase, etc. They anticipated quick, direct action. A query from the AP office in Bern, Switzerland to the Berlin office received a laconic reply: "Hurry up. We leave for the jug." When Bern asked about the possible internment, Berlin responded, "We don't know. All American correspondents have been asked to leave for their homes in Berlin. Bye-bye, old man." Immediately afterward the connection stopped operation.[3] The Nazi bureaucracy was moving toward a resolution.

Lloyd Yates, Dr. Fishburn, Freddie Oechsner, Leland Morris, Francis Cunningham, Ev Holt, Major J. Lovell, Cyrus Follmer, Phil Fahrenholz, Frank Phillips, Pat Conger, Onnie Lattu, Angus Thuermer

That night the Gestapo, which traditionally preferred the anonymous darkness to daylight for any action, began collecting the newsmen. They found Alex Small and Paul Dickson of the *Chicago Tribune* first. As he departed with his grim-faced escort Small cheerfully waved to his wife, suggested that he might see her again, and asked her to take good care of their canaries. At 12:50 a.m. the Germans knocked on the Lochners' door. Showing their identification the two Gestapo men asked Lochner to dress and come with them. They were perplexed when they discovered that he already had his bag packed, indicating advance knowledge of their arrival. Lochner confirmed this assumption with the remark, "Why do you think I am a newsman?" The Gestapo indicated that the arrest was merely a simple formality, and that he would return home shortly. In their unmarked car Lochner met his youthful AP colleague, Angus McLean Thuermer.

AMERICAN PRESS CORRESPONDENTS IN BERLIN

Name	Address	Telephone No.
ASSOCIATED PRESS	Zimmerstrasse 68	17-0295 17-0296
Louis P. Lochner in charge (Wife in Berlin)	Giesebrechtstr. 20 Berlin-Charlottenburg	32-2396
Alvin J. Steinkopf	Lützowufer 11, (Dittmann) Berlin W. 35	21-3906
Preston L. Grover	Budapesterstrasse 25/27, Berlin W. 50	25-4257
Ernest G. Fischer	Uhlandstrasse 169/170 (Grosskopf) Berlin W. 15.	92-2965
Angus M. Thuermer	Giesebrechtstrasse 7, (v. Brederlow), Berlin-Charlottenburg 4.	32-2427
UNITED PRESS	Unter den Linden 43-45	11-5696
F.C. Oechsner in charge (Wife in Berlin)	Hotel Villa Majestic Wilmersdorf	97-7651
Jack Fleischer	Bayreutherstrasse 34 Berlin W. 62	25-2034
Howard K. Smith	Bayreutherstrasse 34 Berlin W. 62	25-2034
J.W. Grigg	Meierottostr. 2, Berlin W. 15	92-3468
R.C. Hottelet	Meierottostr. 2, Berlin W. 15.	92-3468
Dana A. Schmidt	Olivaer Platz 11, Berlin W. 15.	92-5963
Alex Dreier	Olivaer Platz 11, Berlin W. 15.	92-5963
ACME NEWS PICTURES (United Press affiliate)	Unter den Linden 43-45	11-5696
Jean Graffis	Olivaer Platz 11, Berlin W. 15.	92-5963

- 2 -

INTERNATIONAL NEWS SERVICE (Hearst Press)	Dorotheenstrasse 28-29	11-0163
Pierre Huss	Dorotheenstrasse 28-29	11-0163
CHICAGO DAILY NEWS	Unter den Linden 43-45	11-0130
Dave Nicol	Viktoriastrasse 31	21-4170
CHICAGO TRIBUNE	Hotel Esplanade	22-1457
Sigrid Schultz	Tiergartenstrasse 43	26-0547
E.R. Noderer	Hotel Esplanade	21-8181
CHRISTIAN SCIENCE MONITOR	Unter den Linden 33	12-1754
Joseph C. Harsch	Budapesterstrasse 25	25-4257
NEW YORK TIMES	Kanonierstrasse 1	12-7576
Guido Enderis	Hotel Continental	22-0022
Brooks Peters	Berlinerstr. 153 Berlin W. 30.	34-7815
Percival Knauth	Kladow	80-8424
TIME AND FORTUNE MAGAZINES	Jerusalemerstr. 50/51	17-7456
Stephen Laird) lael Laird)	Jerusalemerstr. 50/51	17-7456
SATURDAY EVENING POST	Hotel Bristol	11-0033
Demaree Bess	Hotel Bristol	11-0033
N.B.C. (NATIONAL BROADCASTING CO.)		
William C. Kerker	Wielandstrasse 14 Berlin-Charlottenburg 4.	32-0656
C.B.S.		
William L. Shirer (on leave)-Hotel Adlon		
Harry Flamery	Hotel Adlon	11-0026
PRESS WIRELESS		11-0026
Louis Huot	Budapesterstrasse 25	25-4257

- - - - -

Another group of arrested newsmen included Fred Oechsner, the United Press Chief in Berlin, with his associate Jack Fleischer, as well as Jean Graffis of Acme Press and Ed Shanke of the AP. They were a quiet group, packed into a light truck. The last group assembled by the Gestapo was the loudest. They awakened Ernest Fischer of the AP at 4:45 a.m. with their loud pounding on the door. Ordering Fischer to dress, the three Gestapo men, as with the others arresting Lochner, were nonplused by his nonchalance (he drank Chianti while dressing) and his prior preparations. They escorted him to a truck, where he discovered Joe Grigg, Glen Stadler, and Clinton Conger of the UP; Alvin Steinkopf of AP, and Hugo Speck of International News Service. The last named was highly intoxicated and wildly angry over a policeman's question as to whether he could write or not. Speck refused to believe that the man's concern was more about his sobriety than about his literacy.

Irrespective of their pick-up points the vehicles all took their guests—as they termed them—to the police station on Alexanderplatz. They climbed to the third floor and passed through a heavy metal door sealing a section marked "Secret State Police." A nondescript official slammed it ominously shut behind them. In another room the Nazi officials required them to put their names and birthdays on slips of paper. Thereafter they could exchange stories of their arrest and review their surroundings. The room was a very large one, with a high ceiling, and filled with numerous desks. Dominating the room were the grim pictures of Adolf Hitler, Heinrich Himmler and Reinhard Heydrich. In particular the eyes of Heydrich made them uneasy about turning their backs. Nonetheless the irrepressible newsmen began to relax. Shanke, feeling a sudden cramp in his leg, spread out a newspaper on a desk top and put his feet on top of it. Just as he settled down for a rest, a guard urgently tapped him on the shoulder with the terse reminder, "We have not fallen that low yet."

The time passed slowly without any activity. About 9:30 a.m. Paul Fischer, who had taken a position with the National Broadcasting System after being stranded as a student in Germany, arrived-the last man to be arrested. He had changed addresses and, thereby, had been a frustrating problem to the Gestapo. As Fisher came in a sleepy Speck, feeling the effects of his earlier activities, quietly spread his overcoat on the floor in a corner and stretched out. He was sound asleep when a Gestapo guard discovered him and ordered him to stand up. A bemused Speck accepted the command, reached up, grabbed the nonplused guard's arm, and pulled himself up with the words, "Thanks buddy." The unruly newsmen were creating problems for their captors who seemingly had no idea about the next step after bringing them to the police building.

Daylight on December 11 brought them no relief. Without breakfast, the Americans intensified their complaints. The guards, who also received no breakfast, were just as angry as their guests and even more frustrated by their uncertainty over their unwanted guests. At noon the Gestapo furnished a decent lunch which, when combined with some of the groceries brought by the correspondents, created a more contented atmosphere. The guards, noting some of the canned goods, served as waiters. After finding a radio which one of their number repaired, the journalists sat down in preparation for Hitler's speech. Shortly afterward—and before the Fuehrer's remarks—an officer suddenly ordered them to put on their coats and pick up their baggage. They marched down the stairs and climbed aboard an Army truck, which drove off at high speed. The fact that the Germans had declared no destination caused one American to make a pessimistic remark: "Well, this is the end, boys." However, after a short trip they arrived at the Riviera Hotel in the Grunau district of Berlin.

The apprehensive representatives of the press quickly discovered that the Riviera did not live up to its romantic name. It was a bowl-and-pitcher hotel under military control. The eight fully equipped and armed guards were already present. A minor party official informed them, in rehearsed, if faulty, English, "keep your rooms clean, keep feet off the beds, watch your conduct to avoid a bad impression with visiting officials, arise punctually for meals." The correspondents found, to their dismay, that the steam heat did not work, and that only one room had a stove to provide some warmth for the unhappy fifteen. During the night a radiator had burst and eliminated the central heating. They had missed Hitler's speech and they had accommodations providing little hope or happiness. Supper did not help morale in the least—two slices of bread and some dried wurst.

"wishful thinking"
Alvin Steinkopf

The following day provided additional concerns but Fischer provided one bright spot. He had brought camping utensils for reasons he could not explain, and a small copper tea kettle. It became a major focus for the group, continuously in use for heating water. While breakfast failed again, a lunch of bean and potato soup raised hopes that someone had assumed responsibility for them.

Immediately after lunch some uniformed officials demanded the apartment keys of the single men among the group. Right behind them came Dr. Emil Rasche and Werner Plack of the Foreign Office and a Dr. Froelich from the Propaganda Ministry. They quickly announced that the future of the Americans would be directly reciprocal to the treatment accorded their German counterparts by the United States officials. In response to a journalist's question as to whether or not they had heard anything about his countrymen, Rasche answered, in a significant tone, that he possessed some information but would not make further comment. Froelich confirmed that a state of war existed between their two countries, but refused any explanation of the circumstances. Rasche then added the first words of hope, reporting an official American proposal that the German journalists be treated as diplomats. He inferred that his superiors would do the same for the American correspondents once a mutual understanding was in force.

The German officials departed with the bemused Americans pleased over their notice, but uncertain about its significance. If nothing else the visitors had impressed the guards that their American charges were more important than they had believed originally. Thereafter they were more considerate and attentive.

About 5:00 p.m. a guard called Lochner aside, cautioned him to silence, and let him speak with a visitor—Mrs. Lochner. Through an unidentified telephone caller she had learned of their location and had hastily assembled what she could carry—a suitcase of apples, some cigarettes, and various magazines. She had talked her way past the decent but uneasy guards to provide her husband and his colleagues with a heavenly gift of food, tobacco, and reading material.

That evening, in return for a cigarette bribe, a guard brought them a newspaper with a rendering of Hitler's speech. Lochner read it aloud and then led a discussion about its meaning and purport. They agreed that the Fuehrer was losing his charismatic touch, showing signs of a deteriorating megalomania. In particular they found his skewed history lesson dull and boring, and took his shrill threats against domestic saboteurs as signs of increasing Nazi insecurity. The usual inspirational tone and spellbinding commitment of Hitler's speeches was missing. The newsmen all shared the view that the war declaration would bring universal doubt among the Germans whose knowledge of history, including the outcome of the First World War, would raise considerations totally unwelcome to Nazi aspirations. The Americans went to sleep no more certain of their own prospects than earlier, but happier about their immediate circumstances.

Alex Small

On December 13 Jean Graffis celebrated his thirty-seventh birthday, breaking up some of the growing tension of inactivity. Everyone joined in singing "Happy Birthday" and planning a party that afternoon. They spent the morning trading bawdy stories, singing raucous songs, and otherwise battling boredom. Lunch was a mess of barley broth and rotten prune juice, which most of the hungry newsmen passed up. That afternoon two German employees of the Berlin AP office, together with an official of the German Foreign Office, a Herr Schwerder, brought some additional food supplies donated by various friends. The AP men brought news of a message from Kent Cooper, the general manager of their firm in New York, indicating that the State Department would allow the German journalists in the United States full diplomatic rights, including departure with the legation staff. The news created a festive mood for the birthday.

In preparation for the party several journalists moved four wicker chairs from the reception area to the heated room. When the German hotel commander asked for their return he clarified his orders with the explanation that he could not furnish everyone a wicker chair; it was all or none. Oechsner responded that they would take turns sitting in the chairs. The German retorted angrily that he had given them a good reason for his request; but that failing, he wanted the chairs back where they belonged because that was where they belonged. However, he left, and the Americans simply paid no attention to his demand.

They were busy sorting out the available materials for the birthday celebration. Various people donated wine and a bottle of cognac, which allowed a rudimentary cocktail hour. Fischer began the long process of slowly cooking canned vegetables and meat for fifteen hungry souls. He could only cook small portions. As they prepared a simple ceremony a German official arrived with a brief announcement. Opening with the sentence, "You are released," he went on with instructions that they should return home, pack their possessions, take them to the Embassy, and report there the following morning. With much-enhanced spirits the journalists finished their modest celebration and then caught a train to Berlin, about a thirty minute ride.

Once back in the city they completed their packing, bade farewell to those friends they could reach, and prepared for their departure. Many of them discovered that unknown Germans had looted their supplies and possessions. The blow was a very personal one since the Embassy had only granted them access to the commissary on December 1. Cans of meat, butter, coffee, cigarettes etc., were gone without trace. Many lost their silver, clothing, and other possessions. There was no time, opportunity, or official for complaint. The fortunes of war had discovered them. For some this discovery was sufficient grounds to consume the residue.

The next morning, not feeling their best after a long night, they appeared at the Embassy. The Germans returned their passports in exchange for a statement that no one had lost any personal property. Steinkopf was alarmed to find a waiting police official. In searching the rooms of the journalists the official had discovered a small artillery shell, left by Steinkopf's former roommate as he departed for home. After some confusion Steinkopf successfully explained the situation as a defused souvenir and the official dropped his concern over potential sabotage.[4]

The journalists now joined the other Americans in anxiously discussing their imminent departure from Berlin.

NOTES

[1]Although confined to its subject, a useful study of a journalist's dilemmas and games is Joy Schaleben, "Louis P. Lochner: Getting the Story Out of Nazi Germany, 1933-1941" *Master of Science Thesis*, Journalism, University of Wisconsin, 1967. Shirer's *20th Century Journey*, pp 255-261 contains some insightful comments.

[2]The best account is in Louis P. Lochner, *What about Germany*? (New York: Dodd, Mead, 1942), pp. 360-361, although the story appeared, in somewhat different form, in most American newspapers. Also descriptive is Martin H. Somerfeldt, *Das Oberkommando der Wehrmacht gibt Bekannt* (Frankfurt: Westdeutsche Verlag, 1952), pp. 66, 87. The Americans had arrested five German journalists for what Attorney General Anthony Biddle termed "activity regarded as dangerous to the peace and safety of the United States."

Lochner was among the most interesting members of the newsmen's group. Fluent in both the German culture and language, he had been in Germany since 1921, heading the Associated Press Bureau since 1928. Together with his German second wife, Hilde, he had established an amazing circle of informants and resource people. Lochner was in constant motion, passionately dedicated to his work, and always looking for ways of getting ahead of the competition. He enjoyed the respect of his peers for his skills, although some complained about his accommodations with Nazi officialdom. He wrote some interesting memoirs, *Always the Unexpected; a Book of Reminiscences* (New York: Macmillan, 1956) and left his important collection of papers to the State Historical Society of Wisconsin.

[3]As reported in Oliver Grambling, *Free Men are Fighting: The Story of World War II* (New York: Farrar and Rinehart, 1942) p. 277.

[4]This account comes from Lochner, *What About Germany?*, pp. 361-368; Grambling, *Free Men are Fighting*, pp. 387-388; Alvin Steinkopf, "Diary" December 14, State Historical Society of Wisconsin. Ernest Fischer, "Notes," pp. 1-3. Fischer was a quiet, thoughtful person with an intense pride in the state of his birth, Texas. He had varied and extensive journalistic experience before he arrived in Berlin in 1940. A compulsive writer who never gave up writing, he deposited his marvelous diary, some numbered miscellaneous notes, and a non produced dramatic manuscript on the internment at the State Historical Society of Wisconsin. See also Clinton B (Pat) Conger, "Guest of the Gestapo," *The Quill* Vol. 30, (August 1942), pp 3-4, 14-15.

CHAPTER III

KENNAN TAKES CHARGE

Oh, once we were told that to kick at our fate
Would make our departure a whole lot more late
The Russians had squawked and their Cyrillic squeaks
Had lengthened their 'durance to almost six weeks
If we would keep silent, much better we'd fare
So our minds they are wasting away.

Untitled

On December 14 the entire group of expectant Americans gathered for their departure in the American Embassy. A few journalists had an inkling of their destination but said nothing for fear of embarrassing error. A mistaken rumor could bring serious social retribution, since the group was one of many strangers. The members of the assembly, tired and excited, talked a good deal about very little. While the story of the journalists' adventure, offering the sole insight into the future, dominated discussions, verbal exchange provided an emotional outlet for unspoken concern. Various members of the international community hurried in for demonstrative farewells, showing their personal concern and their solidarity with America.

The most enduring memory of the participants in that day was the unholy mass confusion. Suddenly thrust together in a hastily prepared departure, they lacked discipline, roles, direction, or awareness. The paper leadership of the group was present but not yet accepted. The result resembeled a riot in a bird house.

As Kennan counted noses he found 114 individuals and several pets (including the Smalls' canaries). The range of people embodied a small American community although the educational level (seventy-nine possessed college degrees) was well above the norm. Among them were custodians, doctors, secretaries, dancers, teachers, and musicians, often expatriates with little earlier interest in returning home. They joined a large group of foreign service personnel with a handful of dependents, the military attachés, and the journalists. One, Miss Geraldine De Courcy, was leaving Berlin as a repatriate for the second time. By this time, all the Americans, irrespective of background, purpose, or position, were unified in their desire to return home.

Although everyone (excluding Burgman) reported on time the Germans had trouble organizing the departure. They brought three double-decked buses, six private automobiles, and five army trucks. The massive pile of personal baggage and effects overwhelmed the few baggage handlers, who strained themselves in loading everything on the trucks. Their complaints brought them no reinforcements. At 10:30 the Germans started loading the buses with the internees, with resultant chaos. Despite Kennan's careful mobilization efforts, different groups got entangled with each other. Undisciplined individuals wandered around, seeking their places in the most desultory fashion. While the groups were directed by the disciplined attachés, the latters' experience was much different than that of their charges. Other complications with closing the buildings and transferring funds to the Swiss created further delays.

The cortege finally departed around noon, in intermittent rain squalls, for the Potsdamer Railway Station. One class-conscious observer, not as competent with figures as with opinion, suggested unkindly that the buses carried "ninety-seven Americans and fifteen correspondents" (leaving Mrs. Lochner and Mrs. Small out of either group).[1] Along the way none of the German civilians took the slightest notice of the vehicle column. As they moved past the French Embassy, Mr. M. Fraysse, the French vice consul who had remained behind as custodian, leaned out of a window and waved a large white handkerchief in farewell. As they drove along the silent streets many saw buildings associated with fateful memories—the zoo, the Reich's Chancellory, Leipziger Platz, The Brandenburg Gate - and wondered about the future.

They came into the station through a side entrance. The numerous guards kept them in a single file between the buses and the platform - a serious reminder of their uncertain status. The station officials kept the Americans separated from the Germans although some foreign attaches, led by Captain Hans von Schwerin, the Swedish assistant attaché, pushed their way through the barriers. They expressed fond farewells. The train had a baggage car at the head, followed by three first-and second-class sleepers; then a dining car and four third-class sleepers (one of which served the police and train personnel). At the end was a second baggage car. In contrast to the strain at the Embassy, the loading at the station progressed easily, but, again, the bulk of the baggage (in excess of 1,000 pieces) created delays until 1:15, when the special train departed Berlin.[2] Nearly everyone fell asleep immediately. The excitement and strain of their circumstances over the previous day's activities had exacted a price on their nerves.

Leaving Berlin

The train provided few conveniences. Unfortunately the combination of wet, cold weather and the lack of heat or hot water on the train caused immediate discomfort. The third-class accommodations featured hard board seats without cushions and were extraordinarily dirty. Shortly after departure various bugs began moving about, adding to the passengers' apprehensions. The conditions were so bad that many people understandably sought better accommodations, creating more confusion. Kennan unraveled everything through his forceful personality and organizational skill but found little rest. Complaint was omnipresent and he listened while resolving the soluable difficulties. Although fed in shifts the meals were palatable, especially when supplemented with private supplies. If nothing else, the luncheon menu, headlined Berlin - Bad Nauheim, provided the first official indication of their destination.

Alex Small and his canaries

After an uneventful trip through the mystical Harz Mountains, with only a pause in Goettingen (where those with a sense of history remembered an earlier academic strike for freedom), the train arrived at a siding in Bad Nauheim, a spa (for heart and rheumatism patients) about thirty kilometers north of Frankfurt. It was 10:00 p.m. Patzak and Kennan informed the tired travelers that they would spend the night on the train and must reckon with the possibility of some additional nights. The arrival of local utility workers who connected city water lines with those of the train, supported the idea that their stationary hostelry might be needed for several days. At least the Americans learned that they would be in Bad Nauheim until their final repatriation, and they would eventually be lodged in Jeschke's Grand Hotel. The city itself was an

Bad Nauheim
Kurhalle in foreground

internationally known spa, with many hotels and mineral springs, appealing to the wealthy. The Americans with a sense of history noted the irony that the family of President Roosevelt had enjoyed several summers in residence because of the senior James Roosevelt's heart problems. In fact the future president had briefly attended school in Bad Nauheim and learned some German. In 1895 the senior Roosevelt had contributed to the erection of an Anglo-American church which ultimately contained a tablet memorializing his generous contributions.[3]

view of Bad Nauheim
from the hotel

The next day the group, dirty and uncomfortable, suffering from the foul air created by the overused toilets, shifted from questioning to complaining. Their grumbling did not help the overworked Kennan's temper. He was slowly realizing that the full administration of the internment would fall on his shoulders. Morris, whose interests and experiences were all in the consular area, assumed a very passive role in the procedures. While he was seldom an obstacle in negotiations, administration, or direction, he was not a help either, being most often in his quarters. Kennan was the central authority figure.

Kennan's first happy accomplishment was arranging for walking privileges for his unruly charges. They could stroll around a guarded stretch of pavement 150 paces long. While restricted, this privilege provided some relief from the crowded train.

At least the meals were palatable although the Americans found the tasteless yellow pudding dessert (a nondescript composition of substitute (ersatz) gelatine, sugar, and egg, with a little flour and a touch of vanilla) disastrous. They could not know that the infamous pudding would become the most enduring memory of their incarceration. The sole accomplishment of this tedious day on the train, beyond the walkway, was the accomplishment of the journalists, who got a guard drunk and consequently relieved of his post. They suspected that he had benefited from the earlier plundering of their apartments and the revenge, justified or not, created much happiness.[4]

. . . on a walk

After a day of waiting, on December 16 Patzak finally arranged a visit to the Grand Hotel for Kennan. The hotel did live up to its name in many ways. Designed as a summer-season residence for wealthy individuals seeking "cures in comfort", the building had cost some 5,000,000 gold marks (in excess of $1,000,000) and had opened in May 1912. It had 400 rooms for 210 guests on six floors, but deliberately restricted the number to 180 as an accommodation for those persons seeking larger suites (William Randolph Hearst and Charles Schwab among them).[5]

Grand Hotel
Bad Nauheim

Unfortunately for the Americans and, for that matter, the Germans as well, the glamorous hotel had closed in September 1939 with the onset of the war. The staff (about 200 people) had scattered all over Europe and had lost all contact with their employer. The head chef was in Russia; the chief-engineer in Paris. The hotel director, Gustav Zorn, had lived a lonely existence as the sole inhabitant of the huge structure throughout its closure. None of the hotel's facilities—water, electricity, heat—had functioned during the intervening period, and disuse and neglect without any maintenance had created serious problems. In particular several heating pipes had burst from the freezing winter. Much of the carefully wrapped furniture was in storage, as were the linens, silver, curtains, and all the accouterments. In many respects Kennan found the luxurious structure more a barn than a hotel. Given the permanent closing of the building for the duration of hostilities no one had even considered blacking out the building, establishing security measures, or efficient staffing plans. Obviously the hotel possessed a grand history but was scarcely prepared for sudden wartime occupancy.

Zorn had learned only at noon on Saturday, December 13, that he must reopen his facilities for the internees who would stay for an indeterminate period. With a sudden warning of less than twenty-four hours before the Americans left Berlin and with Sunday, a day when all work was impossible, before him, the director could not begin his efforts until after the Americans' arrival. They were voicing their complaints about the miserable hospitality of Bad Nauheim before he could even initiate the measures required for reopening the facilities. Kennan noted appreciatively the heroic efforts of Patzak and Zorn, which he termed a "tour de force" under highly difficult conditions.

Grand Hotel
on the "River" Usa

Throughout the day Kennan and Patzak puzzled over the room assignments. Kennan, in particular, understood the very real challenges of assigning space to his independent countrymen. But, since he did not know his colleagues intimately, he could not anticipate their individual peculiarities; smokers, snorers, social attitudes, rank order—to say nothing about the characteristics and locations; of the rooms, i.e., their relation to stairs, elevators, public restrooms, etc. In some despair he decided in favor of making the assignments as best he could, and let a subsequent room committee, headed by a military man, make individual corrections. Necessity forced decisiveness. At the same time Kennan understood the human problems of space allocation. Whatever he did the assignments would create acrimonious complaint and provide universal discontent.

Even so the conditions at the hotel forced the group to move in by stages, rather than in a single movement. Accepting that fact meant that Kennan would have to endure constant complaint, both over the transfer period and also for sometime thereafter. Nonetheless the shift of even a few people to the hotel would ease the cramped condition of those left on the train, while giving that group realistic hopes for the future. They would have more space which would lessen their immediate anguish.

Amazingly by that evening the Germans had made sufficient preparations and shifted some twenty Americans to the first floor of the hotel. The conditions were primitive. There were no curtains (which wrought panic among the local German air defense officials), glasses, towels, or other amenities of life.

The private baths did not function, nor was there any hot water. Clearly the hotel could not provide any food service at all. Nonetheless, the fact that the hotel could accommodate anyone was something of a miracle.[6]

The following morning the fortunate people in the hotel met in the lobby and started for breakfast on the train. As they did so a guard ordered them to form in columns of threes, as if they were captured soldiers in a prisoner-of-war camp. Patzak, overhearing the brusque instructions, promptly contravened the order, reminded the guards of the civilian status of the internees, and instructed the guards to avoid such militaristic efforts in the future; they were not prisoners-of-war. As a result the the Americans were allowed to walk at a measured pace, as though they were paying guests rather than wards of the government. Despite the constant attendance of the guards the strollers viewed Patzak's intervention as a tone-setting one auguring well for their brief stay.[7]

The process of transfer placed an immense burden on those people responsible for meal planning. On the train the dining car could accommodate only one-quarter of the group at a time. Since the number of people coming from the hotel and those remaining on the train changed each day, the sittings required much coordination between Kennan's staff and Patzak's group in arranging the meals, providing the guards, and organizing bus transportation after dark, because of the blackouts. The dining room staff—two cooks and three waiters—prepared and served over 400 individual meals each day, in addition to the normal a la carte orders. Other than the dessert, the meals were as good as the cramped train quarters were bad.

While the successful coordination of feeding schedules provided a triumph of joint planning, it also raised a fundamental matter of governing principle. Kennan understood the long range concerns of cooperation with the Nazi officials in relationship to the entire administration of internment. On the one hand, he could choose the justifiable, negative position of refusing all cooperation with the Germans. He possessed adequate rationale, in that the Germans had confined the Americans against their will, that the Americans were innocent victims of the war, and that the Americans had no reason to help their captors in questions of order and discipline. The closure of the American Embassy had completed the official aspect of their mission and turned the Americans into travelers en route home.

Had they chosen this position, Kennan and Morris would have compelled Patzak to deal directly and individually with each member of the group. Also, Kennan knew this position would satisfy the chauvinistic attitude articulated by numerous members of the group. Such a position, perforce, would allow great power to the most insignificant police bureaucrat, giving him personal authority over the most senior American officer. This prospect was not a happy one, in the opinion of both Kennan and Morris and some key members of their staff. They also discussed the issue with the accompanying Swiss representative, Agostino Soldati, Attaché of Legation in Berlin.[8] They decided against such a course of action and in favor of a more friendly attitude.

Thus they cooperated with Patzak as fully as possible, assuming that this approach would increase efficiency on both sides, and that the attitude and support would reduce the excuses for direct interference by Nazi officials. Moreover the pragmatic approach would give the Americans a large measure of self-governance over internal matters and eliminate friction between the Germans and Americans. This policy decision brought immediate results, because Patzak lacked the personnel for maintaining discipline and control of such a large group. Whether he realized the nature of the bargain or not he had little choice, since the alternative position promised chaos. Patzak worked closely with Kennan in establishing an open, direct professional and personal relationship and in organizing the communication links between the two units. In this way they arranged for immediate contact between themselves, but little or no contact between their subordinates, between police officers and individual Americans. Kennan understood the issues.

All internal questions and arrangements, such as room assignments, discipline enforcement, time organization, or complaint resolution, remained strictly an American province. The issues of external supervision, general administration, and material support remained under German authority. In creating a semi-autonomous little America within the frontiers imposed by Jeschke's Grand Hotel, Kennan alleviated many potential problems. At the same time the nature of administrating a confined group for an indetermine time would be difficult. The certain petty squabbles, selfish complaints, and individual requirements assured constant argument. Americans would complain about and to their own officials, who lacked any administrative authority. Kennan accepted the challenge. Given the indeterminate length of their stay, he believed that these issues would surely lead to direct confrontation and probable conflagration between the two groups.[9] His experience in observing other internees made him confident in his decision on governance.

. . . the hotel courtyard

The second group of twenty people moved into the hotel on December 17, allowing the remaining individuals on the train still more maneuvering room. In the third-class cars the relief spared an open rebellion, since the hyperactive vermin had raised welts on some, while the lack of warm water, satisfactory heating, and all washing facilities irritated everyone. Since Germany had sixteen hours of darkness in December and the lighting system broke down frequently, the internees had other complaints. The next day the final body followed, emptying the rancid-smelling train on December 19. The hotel provided breakfast and supper that same day, and thereafter assumed full responsibility for the meal service. In sum, the internees spent varying times of confinement (two to five days) aboard the train. Morris, in the best nautical tradition, was the last to leave.[10]

Lloyd Yates and Everett Holt
a balcony of the Grand Hotel

Finally in the hotel, Morris discussed with Kennan whether to file an official protest against their uncomfortable circumstances, with the hope that the action would remind the Germans of proper behavior. Both men knew that someone in Berlin had made a serious blunder in ordering the internment of so many people without any thought about the necessary logistics. However, they decided against doing anything formally, because Patzak and Zorn were doing their best, under the adverse conditions, to respond to complaints. Official charges could only exacerbate relations without improving the Americans' plight. The sole recourse, which seemed silly, was a demand for returning everyone to Berlin until the Germans could adequately prepare Jeschke's Grand Hotel or another hostelry for occupation. They agreed that a "grin and bear it" attitude was the best option, with the hope that Soldati would voice their complaints with his legation. Once the Swiss government shared the problem with Berlin and Washington, D.C. conditions should improve.

After moving the final group Patzak told Kennan that the Germans would shift the baggage that afternoon. Since he had only three porters, however, they would not be able to distribute the bags in the hotel until after they had unloaded the baggage from the train. Kennan reflected that the baggage pile would further ruffle feelings among the internees and that the train confinement had forced inactivity on the Americans. Calling for volunteers, he let them move the baggage. The American work crew labored with a dispatch which brought compliments from the Germans—and complaints from some colleagues, since there were still numerous Americans totally opposed to any support of the Germans. However, Kennan dismissed the complaints.

Once everyone was in the hotel Kennan began organizing the community for its unknown length and ill-defined confinement. His immediate action was the creation of a room committee, a body with an onerous challenge, since space assignments provided a certain and difficult problem. Many new people were already arriving from other hotels in Bad Nauheim or via other trains. Three journalists (Edward Haffel, Louis Harl, and Philip Whitcomb) appeared on December 17, and Robert Best, a journalist in Vienna, with two relief workers, Martin Lehman and Columbia Murray, appeared two days later. Others would follow. Fully aware of the territorial imperative, Kennan assigned Lt. Col. Smith as chairman, with Lattu and Oechsner as associates.[11] They quickly learned that Kennan's sincerity of purpose was honorable, but that he had not always gambled correctly in his chance assignments. The committee's first sessions were stormy and difficult. One person had a dog of uncertain temper, which necessitated a single room; one had heart trouble, requiring a first floor space; another was paranoid over being near the Gestapo; one man had been a night watchman at the Embassy and could not sleep nights; one person could not tolerate a smoker; another required an open window; another had terrible nightmares, which disturbed his roommate. The committee found, however, that the needed realignments, once people perceived the problem and the trio's manifest sincerity, progressed with comparative ease. While most of the group went along with a measure of philosophic resignation and individual patience, Smith found his knowledge of human beings and their character much expanded by the experience.[12]

Immediately on arrival in the hotel Kennan, with Morris' approval, established a Secretariat to perform as a permanent administrative office. While Morris remained the titular authority, he gave the direct control to Kennan. The Secretariat provided the central function and was responsible for all of the American governance. In a practical sense it established a miniature Embassy chancery. The office drew up and administered all duty schedules for its staff and any subordinate services; it accepted, considered, and resolved complaints from the community; it maintained the official records and controlled the rationing of all supplies to the group; it served as administrator for any miscellaneous funds accruing to the group. Furthermore, and of major importance, the Secretariat handled all of the official contacts with the Swiss legation in Berlin.[13]

Aside from these functions, the Secretariat's fundamental purpose was the implementation of the earlier decision to cooperate with the Germans. Kennan was adamant about preventing individual involvement between the confined Americans and the Germans responsible for them. While unclear about the duration of their stay, Kennan planned for a lengthy residence in the Grand Hotel. If his assumption proved correct, he wanted a firm control of group discipline because he assumed that the boredom, the lack of space, the distance from home and family, and the inevitable friction between people of disparate interests and experiences would bring difficulties. Forced confinement provided many uncertainties for everyone involved in the process. The complexities of collective survival precluded individual freedom and initiative. Kennan wanted an apparatus which would permit group control while providing an outlet other than open conflict with the Germans for letting off the steam created by the stress of enforced confinement. Given that approach Kennan became the narrow neck of the hourglass through which filtered the requirements of the two parties. Kennan provided the direction, coordination, structure, and rule enforcement for the entire community.

Having clearly assumed responsibility for the transfer from Berlin, Kennan had a storehouse of good will built up by his decisiveness. The respect, often grudging, of both his countrymen and the local German officials gave him a decent foundation for authority. While he enjoyed a measure of control over the diplomats, he did not possess any clear rule over the non-diplomats. Kennan was able, through strong will, personal integrity, and open character, to maintain an atmosphere of good faith and cordiality in most contacts. In so doing he eliminated serious complaint in both camps.

. . . courtyard at Bad Nauheim

Beyond the authoritarian Secretariat, Kennan organized several subordinate bodies for designated functions. In this way the administration could keep certain required activities organized with specific responsibilities, locations, and hours, and at the same time provide a regular occupation for several people. Kennan wanted to establish this structure quickly, before any confusing questions arose about who was in charge of what and on whose authority. Therefore, in the course of the first few days, while his charges were busy working out their accommodation with the hotel and their associates, he, employing Morris' imagined authority, organized a large committee sub-structure for the Secretariat. A commissary committee would order and distribute food supplies from Berlin (through the Swiss); a newspaper service would distribute the available newspapers delivered to the hotel; a medical and nursing service would administer aid and assistance to the ill; a shopping service would act as a clearing house for local purchases; and a librarian service would loan books donated by the internees.[14]

Once inside and semi-settled the internees could begin investigating their palatial residence. While the hotel was still in disorder, Zorn's efforts brought continuing progress in returning the building to its former state. The hotel was in a pleasant section of Bad Nauheim, but lacked extensive grounds. Its only garden space was a small, confined terrace abutting a creek, the Usa. The latter became an irritatingly bad pun among the Germans, who enjoyed pointing out how close their charges were to the U-s-a.[15] Inside the building the occupants had only a large lounge area and a spacious writing room, in addition to the breakfast and dining rooms. While these areas were most adequate for their assigned purposes, they were insufficient for large group activities. The staff and the police retained several strategically located rooms for their use. They were as permanent as the people they watched and served.

Dining Room of the Grand Hotel

At the outset the police officials indicated their intention of keeping the internees carefully and constantly under guard. While Patzak accepted Kennan's purpose of avoiding contact between German guards and American internees, he had no intention of losing an American. The Germans established a guard at the hotel's main entrance to control all entry and egress. Guards elsewhere were often understanding and sometimes lax, but this position was one of clear responsibility, and the guards were precise and without sentiment in fulfilling their duties. The only other unlocked door was the rear exit into the garden. While the door was locked at night guards patrolled the area on a twenty-four hour basis. Their loud footsteps, walking back and forth in the snow under the windows, inhibited much sleep.

. . . enjoying the sun

Morris enjoyed the privilege of coming and going without a guard and could move freely through the city. However, he did not avail himself of this privilege, excluding a few rare occasions when circumstances dictated haste. Morris understood that overuse of his singular privilege would one day obligate him to the Nazis and increase his countrymen's suspicions of his motives. Morris knew that the small, confined group would act like the inhabitants of a country village; i.e., there were no secrets, and suspicion, repeated often enough, became fact. If anyone else left the hotel, he always had an accompanying guard.[16] For whatever reason the Gestapo, ostensibly assigned as protection for the Americans, did its best to protect the Germans from any contact with the internees. They did so most successfully.

Before anyone could reflect too much on the situation, Morris issued eight house rules which provided several guidance principles. He cautioned the Americans to behave in accordance with the status of Jeschke's Grand Hotel. They should take care to avoid property damage, and to dress properly (neatly, with men required to wear coat and tie in the public rooms). Since the hotel lacked sufficient personnel to keep all of the rooms tidy, each person must assume that responsibility for his own room.

Underscoring the Secretariat's authority, Morris required that all complaints and any dealings with the Germans be directed to that body for action. In all events Morris cautioned the Americans that their contact with the Germans should be civil but not extensive. The final rule was the explicit caution, "It is in the general interest not to listen to or pass on rumors."[17] The other directions, essential to a well-behaved, orderly community, made obvious sense and were readily accepted, but the final one was as effective as halting the sea with a sieve. In point of fact at least one rumor appeared with the proclamation itself. Soldati, the Swiss representative, let it be known that an exchange proposal was already in Berlin, and that they should be moving in approximately one month.[18]

Under such confinement the Americans lived for and by rumors, polishing and perfecting them until anyone willing to list the "confirmed" reports would have discovered a veritable fleet of identified ships steaming toward Bad Nauheim. Rumors helped pass time while sustaining a person's self-importance in earth-shaking world events. Their experiences took on an untoward significance.

As a good will gesture Patzak quickly initiated a postal service for the internees interested in corresponding with their German friends. He actively solicited their participation. The alacrity of the Germans in encouraging such correspondence made Kennan suspicious, but he could find no explanation other then possible German interest in the relationships between the internees and the natives. Patzak allowed letters to countries at war with Germany as well. The letters passed through German censorship and then went to the Swiss for forwarding through the American legation in Switzerland. As for telegrams, the Americans could receive them, but not send them. Likewise the telephone was off limits to everyone except Morris and Kennan, who could only telephone the Swiss officials in Berlin.

With these structural concepts and rules established or well on the way to finalization the internees could confront the realities of their position. Both sides required adjustments as they arranged operating routines, individual boundaries, group awarenesses. In the interests of hospitality the Germans arranged for barber service, which was welcomed until the barbers gouged their customers three marks as opposed to the normal one mark. The Gestapo excused the barbers. With the first meals the hotel management charged fifty-five pfennigs per glass of milk although retail stores asked twenty-six pfennig for a liter. In this case the arbitrary Patzak agreed with the Americans, and ordered two glasses sold at the earlier price of a single glass.[19] When the Germans needed an electrician, they arrested one for two weeks, and released him for good behavior for completing the job early. When they required two plumbers, they arbitrarily drove around Bad Nauheim until they found two at work, and arbitrarily arrested them, and assigned them to do the work. Likewise, when it became clear that the hotel required another waiter, they employed the same technique. Such summary methods amazed and frightened the internees, who had little direct experience with the political police.

On December 21, Dr. Stewart Herman Jr, former pastor of the American church in Berlin, held an interdenominational church service. He had served in Berlin for six years and, in an effort to accommodate his dwindling flock, had joined the Embassy staff.[20] His first sermon, preached from a teetering platform in the lounge, attracted fifty-three persons. His words were drawn from those of a Pilgrim preacher speaking at Plymouth Rock on the same day, 321 years earlier. Herman emphasized that they should all benefit from their community life in Bad Nauheim but could so only if they contributed something to the group and its welfare. A few holiday carols added to the festive spirit and to the general spiritual optimism among the attendees.[21]

That evening a few select journalists visited Ed Shanke's room (number 228). Although the Americans knew the Germans had banned all radios, the latter did not search for them. Shanke had thoughtfully disregarded these regulations and had brought along a miniature battery-operated RCA Victor radio, approximating a large cigar box (3"x3"x8"), which he concealed in his room. He invited a few carefully chosen people to attend "choir practice" as he termed the activity at 9:00 p.m. (subsequently 10:00 p.m.). Crowding around the radio, they listened to the British Broadcasting Company's news broadcast and then discussed the military situation. Thereafter they relayed the details to their non-participating comrades by word of mouth.[22] This limited link to the outside world was their sole source of reliable information. With that data they were far better qualified to interpret the Nazi newspapers. These were of little substantive value, often contradicting themselves with their changing pronouncements.[23]

Despite the misery of their isolation, the more active insisted on some exercise. Lovell and Lattu, both committed to a physical program, organized a calisthenics group. The first meeting, at 8:30 a.m. on December 23, before sunrise, brought eighteen participants. As they began their enthusiastic activities, in the dark street before the hotel Patzak appeared and suggested that his guards were "worked to death" and that he could not permit strenuous body movements in the dark. Lattu refused the hint, responding that the darkness was no hindrance, since the exercise was individual and non-competitive. One needed only a small area, in any event. Patzak rejoined quickly, "From our standpoint, it is undesirable," and terminated the conversation and the exercise class.[24] Subsequently the Secretariat negotiated a new time, 10:30 a.m., for calisthenics, and also arranged for the use of the sheltered promenade, the so-called "Trinkhalle" across the street, for both exercise and recreational walking at determined times. Despite the annoyance of the ever-present guards, the internees could see some other scenery outside the hotel.

Whitcomb and Lochner
. . . a daily constitution

Following some lengthy exchanges between Patzak and Kennan, the former permitted the Americans to purchase a large Christmas tree (seventy-five marks, or thirty dollars) which they decorated under Lochner's direction on December 24. Even the German police, acquiring the holiday spirit, helped with the ornaments.

Patzak also helped the Americans buy enough wood for a fireplace fire on Christmas Eve. Various individuals organized a holiday gift exchange drawn from the participants' resources, and a brief Christmas eve program. The sum was a universal involvement in preparation which helped the Americans look forward to their holiday far from home.

Morris capitalized on the spirit and allowed everyone to purchase one-half pound of bacon and a carton of cigarettes (total $1.75) from the Embassy stores. His unexpected action gave the internees a major morale boost. He had also arranged for the dispatch of holiday letters and cablegrams through the Swiss, which cheered many who viewed the separation from their families as a severe hardship.[25]

At noon the Americans bade farewell to Soldati, the Swiss observer, who had earned good references as a counselor, listener, and friend. He had an interesting accent and enjoyed playing stuffy pomposity games with the Germans (he always emphasized his residence in the Grand Hotel and his familiarity with the Nazi elite). On his return to Berlin Soldati filed an official report with his government in which he suggested that the transfer had gone well, that the cooperation between the American internees and the German guards was progressing without undue difficulty, and that discipline and morale were high. He did add that Morris sought more details on the repatriation progress, and hoped that no complications would delay the exchange. The note gave a quiet endorsement to the efforts and accomplishments up to December 24.[26] Soldati turned his responsibilities over to the Swiss representative in Frankfurt, Consul Dasen, who would visit Bad Nauheim weekly as liaison.[27]

Dinner on Christmas Eve was a special event. Even the head waiter appeared with a monocle. He also lit the fire, which attracted an immediate crowd, since everyone believed that it would be the last for the duration. The food was undistinguished, but some dubious German champagne improved spirits. Afterwards Graubart served as master of ceremonies for the program. Morris spoke, thanking the German authorities for helping obtain the tree and the community for its discipline and good humor. Graubart gave a humorous speech and then introduced different singing groups who sang holiday songs with some verses. Graubart then read some fake telegrams which included many of the group although the journalists provided the best targets.[28] The program ended solemnly with "O Tannenbaum" and "Stille Nacht."

Thereafter Captain Pickhardt distributed the grab bag presents, a wide range of gifts—hairpins, cigarettes, shoe laces, whiskey, soap, etc. After dinner Zorn made some better quality champagne available, but at appreciably higher prices (the cost was $3.00 for a bottle of champagne and $2.80 per bottle for Rhine wine).[29] The party went on into the morning hours, and most of the group enjoyed themselves.

On Christmas morning Herman held services, giving his sermon on "peace on earth among men of goodwill," and stressing the concept of generosity between men. The ceremony was well attended, although twenty-eight Catholics received permission, with police escort, to attend Catholic Mass not far from the hotel.

. . . winter exercise
a walk in the snow

After a marvelous lunch of roast pork, red cabbage, and potatoes, their first decent hotel meal, the internees went for their daily walk between 3:00 and 4:00 p.m. As the group turned for the hotel, a young woman approached the group, having slipped past a guard. She was Fraulein Otty Wendell, a waitress in the journalists' favorite hangout, the Taverne, in Berlin.[30] Clearly a woman of brassy courage, she explained that she had asked her family in Frankfurt to send a telegram, reporting a family illness. With that pretext, she had travelled home and then taken the local train to Bad Nauheim. Despite the guards dividing the Americans from the German civilians, she sauntered back with the internees, engaging the Lochners in animated conversation. Once in the building, she hurried to see her friend, Alvin Steinkopf. She had brought along several bottles of liquor as a present. Wendell also had news of Berlin, and reporting the continuing decline in public spirit that had followed Hitler's war declaration.

She spent the night with Steinkopf. The next morning she walked boldly into the hotel director's office and asked for employment. In her large bag she had her black dress and white apron as proof of her intent and profession. The director wanted only male waiters and turned down her request. Unsuccessful she left and tried a locked exit, which brought her to the attention of other staff members and the Gestapo man at the entrance, who suddenly remembered her presence the previous day. They quickly apprehended her and the guards hurried her off to Gestapo headquarters under arrest.[31]

Although there was no connection with Wendell's arrival, the Americans coincidently discovered their own problems with even their already limited freedom. On December 26, they turned the door handle for their customary 3:00 p.m. walk—and found it locked. While the German officials had suspended the morning exercise group, pending resolution of some petty differences with America's handling of the German internees, no one had paid much attention. Now, with the front door firmly secured, they were genuine prisoners. Seeking an explanation they learned that American officials had moved the German diplomats in the United States to White Sulphur Springs and restricted their activities which brought reprisals against the Americans in Germany. They would stay indoors until the authorities could resolve the issues.[32]

After some strong words from Kennan the Germans retreated from their overreaction to preliminary news reports. The next day, Patzak's officials gave a forty-eight hour reprieve, in the expectation that someone would resolve the contretemps quickly. The Americans could walk as they had before.[33] Life resumed its normal pace, with the approaching new year bringing anticipation and hope of their release.

Still, certain concerns, fortified by the growing realization that they might winter in Bad Nauheim, spread throughout the group. The first was food. Because of the chaotic initial organization the Germans provided the Americans with more meat and vegetables than were found in the German diet. They tried to provide 150 per cent of the native rations, but usually exceeded it. Nonetheless the Americans found the quantity wanting and the preparation dreadful. Their extensive wrath grew as rations shrank towards the end of December. The prize concoction, served twice a week, was the "Feldkuechengericht," a version of Hessian stew which contained tiny bits of meat (usually listed as the indeterminate "Pochelsteiner Fleish") combined with frozen potatoes, turnips, cabbage, and rutabagas. The cooks cooked it to a pulp in an effort, so the Americans complained, to remove all taste.[34] The ever-present pudding became a universal reason for complaint as well as a constant source of humor. Although unpalatable, it had several advantages: the ingredients came in powdered form, could be easily transported, and remained "fresh" indefinitely.

Lattu, Siewarts, Graubart and "Bobby" Reams

The more observant noted an incongruity about the food problem. While the meals declined in every way, the ambiance of the dining room improved. The dining room of the Grand Hotel became an opulent model of a ship's saloon, dominated by several cut glass chandeliers. All the furniture was on the same scale. The French and Italian waiters wore formal dress, presenting the image of a truly high-class establishment. At the same time the waiters provided some humor. The head waiter, a dour, monacle-wearing German, earned the sobriquet, "Hatchet Face" while a smaller associate, his tails dragging behind him, suffered with "Mickey Mouse." One of the journalists dubbed the room the Sam E. Woods Memorial Hall for Woods, the former commercial attaché in Berlin. Woods, who enjoyed a reputation for setting the finest table in Berlin, found this ironic designation a dubious compliment.

Helga John

While the food remained a major conversational theme, the weather became a more serious cause for concern. The winter's force of cold and snow was clearly approaching. Since the hotel was never intended for winter service, the owners had not invested in a powerful heating plant. The two years of neglect had not helped in the least. Since the system depended on the city's coal-run central generating facilities it suffered from any local coal shortages, while worsening them through its totally unexpected demands on the plant. Because of these strains, the hotel director turned the heat off at 11:00 p.m. and on at 7:00 a.m. As a consequence the rooms were never warm until mid-afternoon, and they cooled rapidly. Some people filled their bathtubs with hot water and slept in the bathroom; others slept in heavy underwear, pajamas, sweaters, socks, overcoats, etc. Some simply visited their friends in interior rooms, which were several degrees warmer, and stayed up late. Others drank red wine for fortification. On December 29, the temperature reached − 13°C and the resultant discomfort seriously threatened morale. The Lattu-Lovell exercise program attracted more and more people, who found it helpful in keeping warm. The temperatures in some rooms reached a high of only 40°F on December 30. For the experienced, this level of suffering was bearable. They were more worried about January.

Despite these difficulties, the group wanted a New Year's party. Graubart performed once more as master of ceremonies, and several people played the piano, while others performed skits. Commander White rendered "My Feder vas a Musiker," which suddenly became Pennsylvania Dutch humor when Patzak appeared in Mufti. No one wanted to offend their official keeper although they found him less formidable in his first appearance out of uniform. Everything ended with "Auld Lang Syne." There was much drinking, happy dancing and a frolicsome mood for most people.[35] Everyone trusted that the New Year would bring them home.

NOTES

[1]Lochner, *What About Germany*?, p. 369.

[2]Kennan, "Report", pp. 7-8. Perry Laukhuff, "Memoirs," p. 29. A story, which remained vivid in many people's minds concerning the hectic final departure rush, concerned a youthful diplomat who exclaimed, "My goodness, there is so much to do around here, if we don't hurry we'll have to board the train without berth assignments according to rank." Reported in some news copy by Ernest Fischer in the Lochner papers.

[3]Rita H. Kleeman, *Gracious Lady. The Life of Sara Delano Roosevelt* (New York: D. Appleton-Century, 1935), p. 163. Mrs. Lochner recalled the story, perpetuated by Emil Ludwig, that the future president had stolen a pencil from the German Kaiser's writing desk during a visit to the absent owner's yacht, *Hohenzollern*. Fischer, "Diary," December 15. For the story, see Emil Ludwig, *Roosevelt, a Study in Fortune and Power.* trans. by Maurice Samuel (New York: Viking Press, 1938), p. 69.

[4]Smith and Lovell, "Story," Part II, p. 3; Stewart W. Herman Jr., "Diary," 14 December 1941. Dr. Herman kindly made the diary available; letter from George Kennan, 3 January 1985. Kennan added that Morris made no difficulties beyond occasionally adding his voice to the complainers' chorus about food - which he knew Kennan and Patzak could not improve.

[5]There was an eerie resemblance to reality in Ford Maddox Ford's novel, *The Good Soldier*, set in Bad Nauheim. Ford has his narrator suggest, "Someone has said that the death of a mouse from cancer is the whole sack of Rome by the Goths and I swear to you that the breaking up of our little four-square coterie was such another unthinkable event," and again about society as a unit, "that long tranquil life," lived by the protagonists in Bad Nauheim, "was just stepping a minuet...The mob may sack Versailles; the Trianon may fall, but surely the minuet - the minuet itself is dancing itself away." Yet life at Bad Nauheim, "wasn't a minuet...it was a prison - a prison full of screaming hysterics...." As quoted in Arthur Mizener, *The Saddest Story: A Biography of Ford Maddox Ford* (New York: World Publications, 1971), pp. 254, 271. The novel is a tragic story of mismatched lives, filled with contradictions and uncertainties as stages in progress towards knowledge.

[6]Kennan, "Report," p. 10; Kennan, "Story," p. 12.

[7]Fischer, "Diary," December 17. One American observer concluded, a bit wryly, "The traditional German efficiency seems to be lacking in effecting arrangements." Smith and Lovell, "Story," Part I, 16 December. See Kennan, "Story," p. 17 for a detailed description.

[8]Soldati was a quiet, observing facilitator who listened more than he talked. He maintained a measure of neutrality but never deviated from his assigned mission in protecting American interests without too much furor. After his labors with protecting foreign interests in the war he enjoyed a fine diplomatic career, representing Switzerland at many international and European meetings and commissions. He finished his career as the Swiss Ambassador to France, 1961-1966. Letter from Director O. Gauge, Bundesarchiv, Switzerland, 16 August 1984.

[9]Kennan "Report," pp. 11-13. "Final Report regarding the Escort of the Group of American Diplomats and Journalists from Berlin to Bad Nauheim" [translation of a report by Mr. Soldati], enclosure to dispatch No 1999, 8 January 1942. File 124.62/289. In his report Soldati pointed out the contrast in organization and discipline between the American direction and the interned Central American representatives lodged in the nearby Hotel Bristol in Bad Nauheim. The latter had made no effort to make some arrangement with the German authorities, with the result feared by Kennan. The Germans gave little respect to the Latin Americans and subjected them to much greater personal supervision. Since the Nazi officials lacked sufficient personnel, the result was continuous disturbance, which merely exacerbated relations to a higher level of anger.

[10]Smith and Lovell, "Story," Part I, 17 December. The constant overuse of the facilities created numerous breakdowns which the Germans could not always repair quickly.

[11]Kennan, "Report," p. 16.

[12]Smith and Lovell, "Story," Part II, p. 4.

[13]The official records contain little material beyond the original housing complaints, transportation conditions, and food and medical requests. With the passage of time, the exchanges narrowed to the actual repatriation issue, reflecting a generally satisfactory relationship. The most notable concern of the Americans was information concerning their status and return home. Letter from O. Gauye, Director, Bundesarchiv, Switzerland, 28 November 1980. Throughout the incarceration in Bad Nauheim the Secretariat handled 1073 communications—511 incoming; 562 outgoing—in addition to the uncounted oral interviews and exchanges. Kennan, "Report," p. 18.

[14]Ibid, pp. 17-21. In three cases, for example, the internees emptied the town of Zivieback - much to the annoyance of the Germans. Kennan, "Story," p. 19.

[15]Fischer, "Notes," p. 12.

[16]The Americans never understood the rationale for the tight security. On the one hand, their sole chance of living in relative comfort and safety depended on the group. Without passports or ration coupons, they could only depend on their friends—who would be in serious trouble for the most modest support. On the other hand, the elaborate precautions begged the issue of many prisoners-of-war, who were then circulating freely in Germany, as were thousands of enemy aliens. On the surface, the legitimacy of purpose in both these groups seemed far less secure than that of the American officials. It was a puzzle which never received clarification. Kennan "Report," pp. 27, 31; Lattu interview.

[17]Copies are in the Lochner papers and in the Fischer diary.

[18]White, "Diary," 19 December.

[19]Fisher, "Notes," pp. 13-15.

[20]Herman, "Diary," 21 December 1941. Subsequently Herman wrote a book, which, given his keen sense of nuance and irony, sadly provides little information on his Bad Nauheim experience. He recounts a simple incident as an example of German methods. Stewart W. Herman, Jr. *It's our Souls We Want* (New York: Harper Bros., 1943), p. xv. His diary provides a marvelous account of the internment.

[21]Fischer, "Diary," Dec. 21. The church program - as are all the subsequent programs—is in the Lochner collection. The service was also a useful collection point for rumors. In this instance, the tale concerned ongoing diplomatic exchanges that the Americans wanted an American vessel, while the Germans desired a neutral one. As well, the Americans purportedly demanded a northern route to Lisbon, while the Germans insisted on a southern route. In reality the entire concept was one written in the wind.

[22]Fischer, "Diary," 22 December; Lochner, *What About Germany?* pp. 370-371; letter from Alvin Steinkopf, 6 January 1981. Shanke replaced the batteries from local resources and which he never revealed. He included some of the attachés but allowed Sam Woods as the only diplomat. Some batteries came through Sam Woods who requested them for his large flashlight. The group had a second hidden radio in reserve but did not have to use it. Smith and Lovell, "Story," Part II, p. 9.

[23]For a short period, the hotel received two French-language papers (Nancy and Geneva) and a German language paper from Zurich. The German authorities suspended these subscriptions in January 1942. Letter from Ernest Fischer, 12 October 1980.

[24]Fisher, "Diary," 23 December; Lattu interview.

[25]On 10 January, the Americans learned that their holiday communications had not left the American diplomatic office in Bern. The explanation was that the office lacked the funds for cabling the messages and letters. Since the internees could not send money out of Germany, they could not pay for their messages. While some of the messages were from State Department people as well as representatives of respectable American organizations, the officials in Bern could find no solution to the impasse. They eventually returned all of the messages—to an understandably sour reception. Fischer, "Notes," p. 32.

[26]See "Final Report Regarding the Escort of the Group of American Diplomats and Journalists from Berlin to Bad Nauheim." File 124.62/289; White, "Diary" 24 December. A second report went to Soldati's superior, Dr. Werner Guber in Berlin and was much more informative. He underscored the hotel problems in Bad Nauheim and faulted German officials (although he complimented Patzak's efforts) for the lack of prior preparations. As well, he called for less obvious police supervision, greater freedom of movement for the internees, and improved correspondence privileges. A copy of his letter found its way into the files of the Sicherheitspolizei. Dr. Maria Keipert, Auswartiges Amt, Bonn, kindly provided a copy of the intelligence interception. Letter of 9 February 1981.

[27]While grateful for Dasen's solicitious concerns about the group's interests, Kennan was not worried about his role. The efficient internal American administration and generally smooth interaction with the German representatives required, in his view, no mediator. Kennan, "Report," p. 35.

[28]One addressed to Oechsner and Lockner went: "HEREWITH IN INTERESTS OF ECONOMY AND GENERAL WAR EFFORT COMBINE ASSOCIATED PRESS AND UNITED PRESS. STAFFS TO COVER GENERAL ACTIVITIES OF GRAND HOTEL BAD NAUHEIM. STOP HIRE I.N.S. REPRESENTATIVES FOR FEATURES ON WOMEN'S DOINGS AND CHICATRIB AND NY HERALD CORRESPONDENTS TO FLASH RESULTS OF BRIDGE TOURNAMENTS. STOP. CABLE TOTAL TEN WORDS DAILY ON *INTERESTING* THINGS YOU DOING AND FIVE WORDS DAILY ON *IMPORTANT* THINGS HAPPENING. STOP. AS SOON AS SITUATION CLEARS, IF ALL STILL YOUNG ENOUGH TO WORK, RUSH EVERYBODY TO WHATEVER POINTS OCCUR TO YOU AT TIME. STOP. ALL STAFFERS WILL [BE] AMPLY SUPPLIED WITH CIGARETTES BY EMBASSY COMMISSARY ACTING ON DIRECT ORDERS SECRETARY STATE HULL. STOP. YOU TWO RETURN TO NEW YORK FOR WELL DESERVED REST AND CONSULTATION WITH PRESIDENT ROOSEVELT. STOP. Copy in Lockner Papers. Not everyone was pleased. White noted, sourly, "It's amazing how pompous platitudes get by—and it is a painful commentary on the lack of appreciation of the majority of this group for what is going on in the world." White, "Diary," December 25, 1942 (sic).

[29]White had earlier noted that "...two things survive from pre-war days; namely the wine cellar and the toilet paper. German war toilet paper is worse than Sears-Roebucks catalogues!" Ibid, 23 December 1941.

[30]For a brief description of the Ristorante Italiano, termed Taverne, where the journalists enjoyed a reserved table, see Shirer, *20th Century Journey*, II pp. 255-259.

[31]This amazing incident is recounted best in Fischer, "Diary" 25, 26 December; Graubart, Lattu interview; telephone conversation with Alvin Steinkopf, 18 January 1981. The Gestapo subsequently interrogated Steinkopf and angrily demanded an explanation. He countered quickly, "Why didn't you protect me? You have got guards posted around this hotel to keep Germans and Americans from communicating with each other. You have failed in your duty - you have failed to protect me against the intrusion of a German girl. After all, you know, our countries are at war and you should not let one of your citizens come in here to see me. I would hush it up if I were you; your supervisors will not like it."

The Gestapo representatives did have red faces. They questioned Wendell in detail again and decided that Steinkopf's suggestion provided the best solution to an embarrassing problem. After a few days, they released her with a harsh admonition about the future. Indeed, she did not return, but she did send Steinkopf, through her own network, several bottles of alcohol. Ibid; Fischer, "Notes," pp. 23-24.

[32]Strangely neither the American nor the German governments kept any records on the internal administration of the internment. Kennan made a report on his own initiative, but the internal documents of the Secretariat are gone. The available records concern external complaints, requests, and demands, but the officials of both countries kept very few records for posterity. Letters from Dr. Maria Keipert, Auswaerteges Amt, 13 February 1980, 27 November 1980. The American files on the Germans are in State Department File 701.6211. While the Americans universally believed that they suffered, while the Germans in the United States lived like royalty, they were not entirely correct. See Margaret Boveri, *Verzweigungen; eine Autobiographie* (Munchen: R. Piper, 1977), pp. 380-401; Fred L. Israel, *The War Diary of Breckinridge Long, Selections from the Years 1939-1944* (Lincoln: University of Nebraska, 1966) p. 233.

[33]Fischer observed, "Sad commentary that two great nations involved in a war concerning millions of lives spend time, efforts and cable tolls arguing the question as to whether 121 Americans held here and about 100 Germans held at White Sulphur Springs should take a stroll. It would seem that they should have other things to do. "Fischer" Diary; 27 December. As he assumed, time had already solved the brouhaha, but the bureaucrats were slow in telling each other. "Treatment of American Diplomatic and Consular Officials at Bad Nauheim" (nd), enclosure to dispatch No. 1999, 8 January 1942. File 124.62/289.

[34]Smith and Lovell, "Story," Part II, p. 4; Fisher "Notes," p. 29.

[35]White, "Diary", 31 December; Smith and Lovell, "Story," Part I, p. 6. Herman, "Diary," 29, 31, December 1941. Frances Nordbye, "Memories," p. 3. White dryly noted, "It's really rather odd, being a prisoner. One drifts into the psychology when the incarceration takes place under diplomatic pressure." White, "Diary," December 31, 1941.

Helga John and Dagfin Hoynes

CHAPTER IV

PASSING TIME

They call it waiting, though the
term is hardly apropos
The folks who've really got to wait
are we; so 'ere we go
We'll blow a hearty Razzberry: loud
epithets we'll yell
And hope that, after we get out,
the whole place goes to Hell!
May Day in Nauheim

The New Year's celebration brought a few headaches, but it did mark the completion of a significant moment in the internees' lives. At the beginning of their stay in Bad Nauheim, plunged into a new world with new companions and new anticipations, they could re-enter the romantic world of their youth: the first dances, the first jobs, and without question the fatigue from too much emotion. The need for new social relationships, the acquisition of territorial awareness made the party a stimulating finish to 1941. In this sense the New year's party did mark the completion of a significant moment in their lives.

". . . a party in the Grand Hotel"

When they had recovered from the celebration they had time for sober reflection. Their lives would be suspended in time until forces beyond their control arranged for their returning to normal pursuits. Until that magic moment they were constrained to grow older in confined isolation, far from the excitement of war, from their homeland, and from their families. They confronted the fact that they were in Germany for an uncertain time period under uncertain conditions and under uncertain leadership. Depending on these forces and the length of their confinement, they faced accommodations beyond the normal order of their lives and their experiences. Nineteen forty-two would be a daunting challenge.

On January 4 Herman preached his first sermon of the new year. He drew a parallel between a person beginning 1942 and a traveler in a railway station confronting a door. The door was closed, and the luggage-laden traveler cannot find a way to open the door while carrying his suitcases. In desperation he hesitated, grabed his bags, and lunged for the door. Through the magic of an unseen electric beam, the door quietly opened for him. Herman's moral was that if his listeners had faith and trust for 1942, they would find a solution over seemingly insurmountable obstacles.[1]

Others in the group also understood the potential problem. They knew that activity would slow, if not halt, the development of a prison psychosis among the internees. Should the incarceration be allowed to overwhelm them, the results were unfortunately predictable and bad. By keeping people busy the internees (now numbering 123, with more additions scheduled from Paris and Copenhagen) could avoid the consequences of boredom, depression, and above all, internecine strife. The more creative people, under Kennan's leadership, began searching for various activities. They could be residents of Bad Nauheim for a long time.

Doris Lawson
Helga Smyser
Werner John

Unquestionably the most successful collective endeavor was education. In January a small group organized a school system which would take advantage of the group's expertise, while providing authentic opportunities for personal advancement. Perry Laukhuf of the Berlin Embassy, a Harvard graduate who had taught at Sweetbriar College, became the first president of the "University in Exile." He organized several courses, most of them in languages. His formalistic approach, as well as his limited conception of the undertaking, did not achieve universal acceptance, and, on February 6, he cheerfully surrendered his post.

His replacement was Phillip Whitcomb, a Rhodes Scholar who had turned to journalism. He had served as a Paris AP correspondent and was a man of creative imagination and infectious enthusiasm, with an intense determination. While many of his associates thought at first that the Bad Nauheim confinement had driven him over the edge of human understanding, they were quickly caught up in his consuming, optimistic commitment to education. Whitcomb created Badheim University (founded by Ichabod Badheim IV at some undetermined time in the past). He served as President (with Laukhuf as President Emeritus), with a Board of Governors and appropriate deans. As part of his development program he passed out a questionnaire to all the internees asking about their teaching skills, professional experience, and individual intellectual interests.

The prospectus for Bad Nauheim University included a motto "Education of the ignorant, for the ignorant by the ignorant shall not perish from the face of the earth" and on the observation:

"My Children, that outer world
—into which someday you will
enter—is clogged with the
thickets of ignorance.
only with the sword of knowledge
can you cut your way.
Here in these sheltered precincts
you can forge that sword."

Whitcomb divided his teaching corps into eleven faculties and organized seventeen offerings for the first session. There were a wide range of subjects: Languages (English, French, German, Russian, Spanish), Phonetics, Russian History, Civics, Bible Study, Physical Education, Tap Dancing, Philosophy, etc.

His prospectus contained some humorous gibes about the internees' uncertain condition: "Wholesome meals in cheerful surroundings are provided on the University premises," and "Arrangements have been made for all students to live on campus in homelike surroundings conducive to concentration on their work."[2] Whitcomb's constant efforts brought surprising interest and gratifying progress among the student body. The fourteen instructors assembled some 228 pupils (most participants took more than one class). George Kennan attracted the largest enrollment for his Russian history course (sixty) while Telegraphy had the lowest enrollment (two—Graubart and White). Throughout, however, the enrollment supported Whitcomb's enthusiasm.[3]

Leon Parker
Louis Harl
Frances Sieverts

As part of his program, Whitcomb established a Department of University Extension, which provided lectures every Friday evening. These formal presentations were devoted to subjects of general interest in which various individuals possessed some expertise. The presentations included an extraordinarily wide range of topics including the American Navy and Army, newspaper work, travelogues, operating a submarine, etc. In virtually every case, the speakers attracted an audience. The same department provided briefer talks—twenty minutes as opposed to forty minutes—on travel subjects, geography, sports, and subjects of broad, general interest, every Monday, Tuesday, and Thursday night.[4]

The general program created much participatory enthusiasm, and the reading room filled with language sessions, study practice, group activities, and arguments over the validity of various presentations. While colds, the frigid weather, and personal spats occasioned periodic absences, dedication remained very high. People entered into the spirit of the school and enjoyed the participation and learning.

As promised, Whitcomb organized a class day for the end of the instructional period. At the ceremonies on March 28, he presented 123 certificates of completion, all appropriately printed, signed, and ornamented with a large gold seal. As part of the program, Whitcomb organized an evening of reveling. Kennan,

BADHEIM UNIVERSITY

THIS IS TO CERTIFY THAT

Helga John

HAS SATISFACTORILY COMPLETED THE COURSE IN

American Constitution

OFFERED BY "BADHEIM UNIVERSITY" DURING THE SOJOURN OF THE AMERICAN GROUP AT BAD NAUHEIM, 1941–1942

MARCH 20, 1942

INSTRUCTOR

PRESIDENT

K/0717

exercising his authority in the Secretariat and censoring some material, dampened some spirits somewhat. Whitcomb disregarded the concern and designed a class yell:

Sprudel doodle cha
Badheim Pudding, USA
Rah, Rah, Rah
Heraus! (begone)

While Kennan excised the final word, believing that it might unduly irritate the Germans,[5] he could not, nor did he try to halt the giddy foolishness, which proceeded in full mockery. The class song opened with:

Oh, Badheim, Mother of Learning,
Dear Badheim, Varsity free
For Thee will ever be yearning
The heart of the internee

and progressed through several verses. Commander White wrote a poem for the occasion, which included the bittersweet observation:

Our shiny new diplomas tell
How work improves the brain
But we've to learn a whole lot more
Ere we get on a train.

Angus Thuermer provided the oration in a marvelous parody of such high school commencement addresses. He observed:

> Tempus Fugit - what is more fitting than to begin this evening's short series of remarks but with that Latin phrase, 'Time flies...and flies, and flies, and flies—

Fellow classmates, you will remember when we arrived here, green as twigs and twice as sappy, unknowing of the virtues of patience, which we have taken now so truly into the very narrow of our souls. Yes, those days are gone forever. At first we strained, unwilling as colts, until those words of Prof. Wurlitzer, "he who waits, waits," were revealed to us in their full significance.

For many a student here at Badheim has applied himself to his books so steadily that it is no wonder that the newest of all words in our language—'Librocupicularistj' (from the Latin, Libro - 'I read', cupicular-'in bed') has here first come into common usage.

The exercises concluded with the words of the famous poet and student of Diesel engineering, Col. Ezekiel J. B. Witherflanks Droopsaddle:

'Breathes there the man with soul so dead,
Who never to himself hath said
I'll close the book,
And go to bed...

These words brought a mighty cheer and the beginning of a happy party celebrating the festivities.[6]

Whitcomb started a new program immediately, with twenty-seven courses scheduled, but the arrival of Spring, increased reports of impending repatriation, and increasing morale problems combined against another success. Nonetheless, his efforts accomplished a great deal in bridging the low point of the internment and maintaining the group's psychic stability. The University and its ancillary activities kept the group's interest, while providing many topics for talk.

Another aspect of the activity program was entertainment. In December the holiday programs—Christmas and New Year—were informal, spontaneous enterprises. Subsequently a formal committee appeared to organize the programs. There were several participants, but Fred Oechsner usually provided the creative and motivational drive as well as discovering and producing unknown talents. The entertainment committee chose Wednesday and Saturday evenings for their varied productions. Wednesdays were normally for games—horseracing, bingo, bridge, treasure hunts, etc. Since no-one forbade gambling, many internees participated in penny-ante wagering with gusto, and celebrated their successes as if they were in the Baden-Baden Casino. The games provided a way to participate for those who could not involve themselves, whether because of age, lack of talent, or interest, in other activities.

"... Holiday entertainment"

Saturday night was much different. Oechsner and his associates created amateur nights with singing, music, costume balls, etc. The performers varied in talent. Mary Ann Kulmer (violin) and Charles O'Neil (piano) were professional performers while others were more enthusiastic than skilled. Numerous dramatic skits provided some comic relief, but the eyes and ears of the Secretariat were always alert to statements that might offend German feelings. Nonetheless these harmless burlesques allowed the internees to mock their membership and release some of the anger and frustration. Lochner organized and trained a choir of twenty-four, which he looked upon as a greater achievement than memorizing the American Constitution for his civics class. Following the program there was dancing—sometimes with a record player, sometimes with a piano player (there were several in the group). In the tradition of American society, Saturday night was the time for losing the week's problems. In Bad Nauheim, this usually meant staying up late, amid much merriment and noise. Societal needs found acceptable resolution. Amazingly, at least three-fourths of the group participated as performers or organizers.[7] This number of participants helped keep the group unified, developing few cliques or public jealousies.

"Recital" - Kulman, O'Neill, Herter, Hofstra, Knapp

Muriel Moynihan & Bobby Reams

Many of the entertainment efforts found publication in a locally created newspaper. Morris asked Lochner, as the ranking journalist, if he might organize an internment paper as a way of informing people of these events. The idea of printing such a newspaper engendered much discussion among the correspondents. Morris had intimated that the Secretariat should "review" the copy before it went into print. For some of the newsmen who had suffered under and struggled against Nazi censorship, the mere suggestion of American review was too much.

The editorial and production staff of "The Bad Nauheim Pudding"

The argument helped fuel mutual suspicions between the journalists and the diplomats (termed "dips" by the former), but they finally resolved the issue in an uneasy, ill-defined understanding. With that the participating newsmen elected Ed Haffel of the Paris *New York Herald Tribune* as editor, with Angus Thuermer and "Pat" Conger as his assistants. Haffel, following some strenuous debate, persuaded Morris and Kennan that the Bad Nauheim Pudding was a meaningful title which the internees would enjoy, without directly insulting the Nazi bureaucracy.

Thereafter came other problems. The paper, purchased by the Swiss in Berlin, would not work easily in the mimeograph machine. It also contained an abundance of static electricity, which made handling a challenge. Struggling with staff problems, supply uncertainties, and miscellaneous concerns Haffel postponed publication until he had everything in place. Ultimately he organized enough reportorial talent, settled the priorities and published volume 1, number 1, on February 7, 1942.[8] It effusively promised weekly issues as long as the group remained in Bad Nauheim, while underscoring the fact that it was the sole American newspaper published in Europe (with the largest English-language circulation (132) on the continent). The publication contained a potpourri of news behind the lead article which trumpeted the latest information on repatriation.[9] The more substantial information suggested that the local waters were good for everything except chilblains, bad colds, and homesickness; that the internees' reading interests centered on detective stories; and that the hotel was operating with a staff of 60 rather than its pre-war 180. The reporters had obtained the statistics of the Americans liquid consumption thus far during internment, which, as of February 6, was 12,287 liters (mineral water, 4,785 bottles; ten barrels of beer or approximately 400 liters per week; and 3,000 bottles of wine). They had also worked out the home states of the group (New York, with twenty being far ahead of second place, Pennsylvania, with eleven). The paper also provided tips on collecting cigarette butts, purchasing items at the general store, and using the "Dawn Patrol shoeshine boys" (two ambitious young men who polished shoes for two marks per week).

The following week the Pudding appeared with a new lead story reporting the possibility of an Italian steamer, *Conte Grande*, taking them home. The reporters were obviously searching for news. They reported delays in Embassy food shipments, the status of University enrollments, various housekeeping matters, and the number and kinds of pets kept by the internees. Clearly life in confinement did not provide much scope for journalistic enterprise.

On March 3 the third issue of the *Pudding* brought on a major controversy. It reported that the Swiss Counselor of Legation in Berlin, Dr. Werner Zuber, had arrived that morning with the news that the Americans would be leaving by the end of the month. He announced that the American and German governments were in agreement on the repatriation proposals and that the internees, together with the Central Americans, would be on two trains. He added that the problems of crossing Spain remained troublesome, but not impossible. The paper further reported Zuber's idea that the group would probably be in Lisbon for several days, awaiting the arrival of the ship carrying the German internees from the United States.

The *Pudding* appeared at 3:00 p.m., with electrifying results. Since the Secretariat had approved the report it legitimized the content. They were going home! But, when Zuber read the announcement, he suddenly decided that the printed word might not be correct and retreated from his position. By 3:30 Kennan had reporter Glen Stadler running through the hotel with a list of the internees, confiscating the entire issue.

EXTRA EXTRA EXTRA EXTRA EXTRA EXTRA !!!

THE * BAD * NAUHEIM * PUDDING

***

Vol. 1, No. 3 | Grand Hotel, Bad Nauheim, Germany | March 3, 1942

MARCH DEPARTURE PROBABLE!

SWISS AUTHORITIES BELIEVE U.S., CENTRAL AMERICAN MISSIONS WILL LEAVE BAD NAUHEIM FOR LISBON ABOUT END OF THIS MONTH

****

Two Trains With Sleepers Planned For Trip Across France; Group Probably Will Cross Spain In Smaller Sections; Budapest Group In Lisbon; Rome Group Hopes To Go Soon

There is a "strong probability" that the American group at Bad Nauheim will leave for Lisbon "around the end of the month," according to information given group officials this morning by Dr. Wernes Zuber, counselor of Legation assigned to the Schutzmachtabteilung of the Swiss Legation in Berlin.

Group officials however added that no fixed date has been set although the last week in March is considered likely.

Dr. Zuber arrived at Bad Nauheim early this morning and since then has been in conference with Mr. Morris, Mr. Kennan, and M. Caillat-Bordier.

Agreement has been reached in principle between the United States government and the German government on the exchange of diplomats at the earliest feasible date. Dr. Zuber indicated that the German government is anxious to have the American group leave Bad Nauheim so that the occupied hotels could be turned over to other guests. The Reich government also has expressed the desire to bring its own officials home from the United States at the earliest possible date.

Technical transportation problems, which had loomed as a possible difficulty to be surmounted in removing the Americans from Bad Nauheim, reportedly have been solved, and the Reichsbahn presumably will be able to put sleeping coaches at the disposal of the group.

The train leaving Bad Nauheim will travel in two sections, inasmuch as the group will include the Central American diplomats living in other hotels in the city. The entire contingent will number "well over two hundred."

Group officials emphasized that although the Swiss authorities take an optimistic view of the prospects for early departure, no hard and fast dates have been given, nor have definite and final arrangements been made.

...t the conference between Dr. Zuber and the group officials the pro-
...ross Spain was raised. In that country
...would have to travel in s...
...unable to ...

Some noted the irony of double censorship; i.e., that the *Pudding* had accepted Secretariat's control in the first place and then paid for its error in judgment. Even the heavy-handed Nazis did not censor their own censored material. A frustrated Stadler, unable to convince the Secretariat that he had recovered all the copies, resorted to face-saving subterfuge. He quietly obtained the original stencils, ran off sufficient extra copies, and turned in enough of them to satisfy Kennan and Morris.[10] The entire affair confirmed the worst fears of the newsmen.

The expected issue of March 7 proved to be the final one. It provided a "Who's Who" of the group, with brief biographies of almost everyone. That service, combined with the clear *faux pas* of Zuber and the Secretariat, finished the usefulness of the Pudding which died quietly. The official reason was shortage of paper.[11] The journalists, however, perceived the confiscation as one of political expedience - and the first such action in a century of American history. While the explanation was transparent, other group concerns and interests obscured the contretemps. In the final instance, the journalists were far fewer in number with less influence than the diplomats—whose command lines were clear.

German Troops,
from the Hotel balcony

Despite these sincere, and very successful, battles against boredom, the stress of daily existence extracted a price. For the internees the key issues of early 1942—beyond repatriation itself—were food and warmth. With some salient, and therefore memorable, exceptions, the food, in both quantity and quality, remained abominable by American standards. In the beginning the uncertain German control, unclear duration of the internment, and unknown reciprocity concerning the Germans in America worked in favor of the Americans. They received 150 percent of the German rations and a disproportionately liberal quantity of meat and fats. Even this relative largess was a shock to the Americans, who were used to a richer diet.

With the new year, the Germans curtailed the internees' diet even more, reducing their rations toward the normal native levels. Since the cutback came at the same time as the full force of winter, the result was a collective scream of protest. Longing for more, individual Americans counted their vegetables, raged over a minuscule piece of meat, and watched each other's plates like wary vultures. Tales about special favors enjoyed by Morris and the senior diplomats were commonplace and believed without any evidence. The incongruity between the formally dressed waiters in a grand dining room and the disappointing face was no longer a point of discussion. Since the more thoughtful had emptied their Berlin larders and brought something with them, they could fall back on their supplies as a supplement. Morris, through the Swiss, placed commissary orders, which helped somewhat in staving off insurrection, but the orders also created unwarranted rumors of favoritism and their delivery dates could not be counted on.

In mid-January, 1942, the food the Germans supplied to the internees reached parity with the normal German diet. The Americans learned to be careful of thinking that matters could not get worse. The meals suddenly had more starches (bread, potatoes, and cereals) and fewer meats, vegetables, and fruits. At the same time the internees confronted the reality that they might, indeed, stay in Germany for a long time. Rumors hinted the possibility that they were in Bad Nauheim for the war's duration. Food then became even more important, because the internees feared malnutrition and health problems. The combination of weight loss and fear brought lower vitality and vociferous complaints over the hunger pangs plaguing every stomach. Dreams were all about food. For Kennan the disputes over food were the most disruptive concerns of the entire internment.

"... winter exercises"

Although all of the Americans complained individually about the food at every opportunity, Kennan could not find a unified group feeling on how they ought to respond. Opinions were 180 dgrees opposed to one another. Certain vocal people called for harsh, direct demands to the German authorities, requiring the food service a first--class American hotel (with realistic retaliation threats against the Germans in White Sulphur Springs as the ploy). Others, while they complained about their diets, found a protest inappropriate. They thought it shameful that the Americans, who had no required activity, could not survive on the rations accorded hard-working German citizens. For them, a protest was both undignified and wrong. Many took umbrage over Kennan's personal views. As one with some stomach concerns, he ate a restricted diet. Envy and anger joined forces. Nonetheless, everyone was consumingly hungry.

A typical breakfast consisted of ersatz coffee (with an overpowering barley taste), two thumbnail pats of butter, ersatz jam, and two rolls. Lochner pointed out that the latter were "...so soggy that one of the more artistic of us would always scrape out the middle section which was like putty and shape and mold it into the prettiest statues."[12]

Lunch and supper varied because of local rationing and distribution problems. Twice a week the cooks provided the roundly denounced "Feldkueche." On meat days, each person received three ounces of meat, often prepared like "fried iron." On meatless days they had vegetables and potatoes, the latter often prepared in varying shapes and forms, depending on the cook's creativity and interest. All of the meals came with the pudding (Griesspeise) which most internees thought was a curse owned and patented by the German Dye Trust.

For Kennan and Morris the volatile situation begged for solution. They brought together representatives of the various constituent groups - military attachés, journalists, diplomats (including the various city representatives from particular cities - Berlin, Paris, Copenhagen) - for consultation, exchange of opinion, and recommendations. After some thought Morris and Kennan worked out a strong protest, which they confirmed with the members of this council. They directed their note to the State Department, through the Swiss representatives.

Before they could get a response, the Germans doubled the American rations to 200 percent of the normal civilian allotment. Concurrently the preparation improved to the point where the food was at least edible.[13] Patzak was clearly making greater efforts to find eggs, fruit, fish, and fresh vegetables. The arrival of spring eliminated the frozen agricultural products. While meat was never plentiful, it ceased being an overwhelming issue. As well, the internees had adjusted themselves to a different diet, although some continued to complain out of habit more as a psychological outlet than a fundamental need. With the improvement in the food came renewed hopes for departure, which further ameliorated some of the internees' attitudes.

The other fundamental concern in January was heat. While the internees had had warnings in December that the Grand Hotel lacked the plant and the coal for proper heating, they were largely unprepared for January's freezing blasts. Temperatures dropped below zero degrees fahrenheit, and the continuing coal shortage in Bad Nauheim precluded improvement. The internees stuffed newspapers in the window cracks, slept in all the clothes they could put on, and wandered into the dining room wrapped in an assortment of blankets, coats, etc. Even the formal Morris retreated on his injunction concerning neatness. He did, however, protest once more to the Swiss that the Germans should improve the heating.

Once more, the result was almost instantaneous adjustment. Patzak approved a fire in the fireplace and obtained the wood for it. Simultaneously the radiator temperatures improved dramatically. The explanation, which the internees accepted as true, was that Patzak had summarily commandered coal from a neighboring town. Whatever the reality he and his Gestapo techniques received full credit for the fact that the heat was suddenly on throughout the night, and for more pleasant heat levels.[14] This solution and the arrival of higher outdoor temperatures in February made the issue academic. The complaints disappeared without comment or note.

By January the hotel was able, thanks to Zorn's efforts, to reach a normal operating pattern. While unable to provide its full range of pre-war services, the staff did give the Americans a wide range of amenities. Because of his personnel shortage, Zorn restricted services to general cleaning, bed-making, and the dining room activities. After a month's delay, he provided a laundry service for those individuals with their soap ration coupons. Many of the internees, planning for a two-week incarceration, had given these valued slips of paper to German friends. Since the coupons were good to February 1 they created some discomfort until everyone drew a new set from the local authorities. Thereafter Zorn's service functioned very well.

Zorn offered room service, but lacked any convenient bell-ringing arrangement. In February he organized pantries on two floors, which eased this problem considerably. Various members of the group, including Morris, took many meals in their rooms. The hiring of people for the elevators allowed Zorn to add this function to the hotel's services. With more heat, more generous meals, and more amenities Zorn provided an improved atmosphere for the rest of the incarceration.

"Fun in the snow"
Bob Stutz, Helga John, Helga Smyser, Doris Lawson, Werner John, Ursula Nett, Gladys Anderson, Francis Sievert

Nonetheless many internees did their own laundry. Most of the men soaked their clothes in the bidet and then stretched the shirts on hangers for drying. The more experienced souls slept on their trousers—a system learned at West Point and passed throughout the Army. In the absence of any hotel employees to do ironing, the internees established their own duty roster for supervisional work in the ironing room and controlling appointments. The Secretariat had undue concerns in this area because the equipment was always unreliable, due to over-use and accidental dropping. Many smokers, male and female, became semi-skilled ironers in trade, as cigarettes fell into limited supply. Patzak could not avoid involvement, either, since a burned-out or broken iron was a serious matter. He was on call, whenever the single hotel iron ceased functioning to obtain repair or replacement.

As the internees settled into their rhythmic patterns of survival they had time for concern about some luxuries. With sufficient food and warmth, the lack of tobacco and liquor became matters of concern. There had been enough cigarettes in the Berlin commissary stores to provide fourteen cigarettes per person per day. Unfortunately several thousand disappeared en route to Bad Nauheim and, with extended boredom, many smokers increased their habit and shortened their supply. An oft-quoted Berliner's observation put the issue in perspective: "Since the heavy snow filled the gutters, my source of tobacco is covered up." Gradually the smokers identified themselves by smoking the cigarettes as short as possible, giving their fingers a toasted brown color. Pipe smokers, without a ready supply source, had greater challenges and became adept at cleaning ashtrays of the butts, which they then broke up for their pipes. These "snipe" hunters became legends in their own time for their skill.

Anticipating a short internment most individuals who had brought along liquor for their confinement consumed it in short order. In about three weeks most of the Berlin supply of alcohol was gone. Thereafter the dedicated topers could purchase wine and champagne from the hotel cellar, which was expensive (room service was available for those of means), or seek out those individuals with greater patience and less thirst.

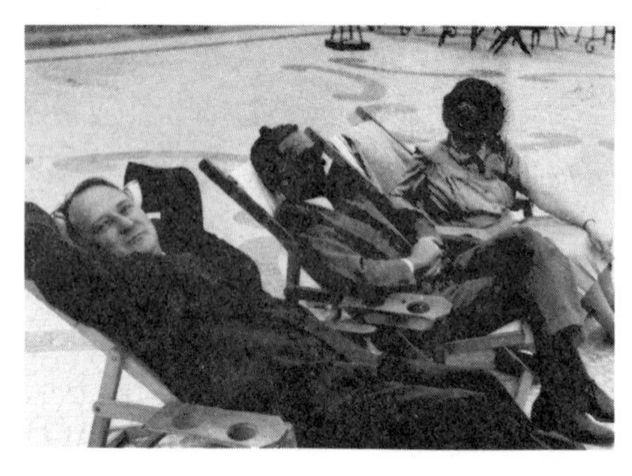

Sam Woods, Eugene Hinkle, Mrs Woods

For a brief moment relief seemed in sight. Because the internees did not have a Catholic priest in their number, the twenty or so Catholics sought and received permission to attend the small church across the street (with proper Gestapo protection). The priest was not enamored of Hitler, and his American parishioners enjoyed his veiled gibes at the Nazi leader, which passed over the heads of the uninterested guards. In their attendance at Mass the Americans intermingled with the Central American diplomats, who attended from the Bristol Hotel. As they knelt together they could exchange rumors and experiences. Both parties soon discovered that the Americans had more tobacco than their Latin neighbors, but limited liquor. The Central Americans, on the other hand, had left Berlin after the Americans and possessed ample liquor supplies, but limited cigarettes. Obviously both sides understood the barter system and quickly established a scale for exchange.

Thereafter the partners would kneel next to each other during the service and quietly swap a carton of cigarettes for a bottle of cognac or whiskey. For the fortunate these meetings changed the name of the church to "The Catholic Church Bourse." As word inevitably circulated among the Americans of this trading venture, attendance at Protestant Sunday services fell off, with a concurrent increase in the number crossing the street. As they noted the developing missionary trend, the Gestapo ordered two Sunday Masses: one for the Americans, one for the Central Americans. Attendance promptly returned to earlier levels.[16]

Brewster Morris, Mrs Nina Reidel
A. Ostertag, Muriel Moynihan
Philip Fahrenholz

The close confinement of individuals over several months impeded their contact with life around them, eliminated their normal sources of occupation and amusement, and challenged the sense of basic familial bonding. Isolated in Bad Nauheim under the watchful, threatening eyes of the feared Gestapo, the individuals required their own control system. Obviously Kennan's understanding of the problem and decisiveness in creating the Secretariat provided immediate form and structure at the very outset. Nonetheless, the arbitrary assumption of authority by Kennan and Morris complicated discipline and individual self-control. The members of the diplomatic community might chafe under their control mechanism as for their participatory role in that administration, but they understood the organizational chart as well as its potential influence on their future careers. For those not serving in or responsible to the Foreign Service or Embassy staff, the power vectors were different. The circumstances of internment forced their voluntary surrender of independence in the interest of group order.

Capt. Schroeder, George Kennan, Robert Reams

The internees, even the non-diplomats, accepted the Kennan-Morris leadership in determining proper conduct, problem resolution, contact with the German authorities, and guidance in meeting the myriad challenges of their existence. The fact that they did so, with much grousing but without defiance, testified to Kennan's skill and the paradox of their position, i.e., they enjoyed a confined, yet acceptable, position in a world at war. Part of this generally smooth sense of order, however, was the occasional aberrant behavior by individuals.

Probably the most discussed behavior was romance. The internees, in some respects, were similar to the survivors of a shipwreck on an island. Instincts threatened conventionalities. Several "couples" developed during the confinement. These "couples" spent their free time together, walked together, sat together, and manifested a "steady" linkage. Some of these relationships suffered prompt rupture when the mate of one member suddenly joined the group from another station. In one case the recently arrived wife of one such duo complained formally to Morris about her husband's "friend" (which caused hilarity, since the couple had been married some twenty-five years, and the wife was several sizes larger than her husband). After repatriation four marriages came to fruition, and at least one serious liaison occurred, but the majority of the relationships, while mildly flirtatious, were not that serious.[17] The major administrative problems came from married couples who could not get along with each other and lacked the discretion of the "couples." One large woman wrapped a lemon in a stocking and hammered her smaller husband with it. They used different rooms thereafter, but their actions provided merriment among their group. Other married pairs suffered their difficulties as well and, since secrets were not possible in such cramped circumstances, provided enduring conversational subject matter.

Among the more memorable incidents in discipline exchange were the Indian dancing-ping pong wars, the fragmented spitoons, and the kite flying-weed picking conflicts. In the first of these the American bridge players, who did not give up until the playing-cards wore out, had their small corner for their games. Next to them was the German police ping-pong table. Naturally the intense card players complained about this noisy assault on their concentration. The Gestapo paid limited heed until Charlie Smith, a Yakima Indian stranded in Europe by a failed entertainment company, started a class in Indian dancing—on the second floor, directly over the Gestapo's breakfast room. This loud foot-stomping created immediate protest. Before the conflict could escalate into war, Kennan arranged a new location for Smith's group in return for the Gestapo's promise to curtail their ping-pong noise. This incident went down in the internment annals as the sole Indian skirmish at Bad Nauheim.[18]

The regular dance on March 6 offered certain party–goers a particularly festive occasion. They celebrated with much drink and general merriment into the early hours and shouted Kennan's angry injunction for peace and quiet. Led by some rowdy journalists, the group enjoyed singing and shouting back and forth until someone (there are several candidates for the creative individual, but none of the participants could remember exactly who it was) noted the large, ceramic spittoons in various corners of the hotel. They were unused relics of past times when visitors, most often Americans, employed them. One of the more spirited celebrants organized an impromptu football contest, using the spittoons as a substitute for the ball. The players dropped several on the floor and then sailed an errant pass over the railing. Plummeting from an upper floor, it smashed into thousands of shards with a thunderous explosive sound. It awakened a frightened police guard, who thought an American bomber headed for Frankfurt had targeted the wrong city, and several of his fellow guards who thought the noise a call for rebellion.

The next morning, an embarrassed Kennan apologized for the incident, telling Patzak that it stemmed from a "prison psychosis," whereby violence resulted from confinement. He then ordered a ban on serving wine in the rooms and cancelled the dance for the next Saturday as punishment.[19]

In April, with better weather, the group received permission for external walks. Virtually everyone availed himself/herself of this opportunity for a walk in nature. Toward the end of the month some of the internees from Paris picked dandelions and made a green salad, much to the envy of their fellow internees. Unfortunately their timing was not the best. They did so just after someone had tossed a bottle out of a second story window, narrowly missing a patroling policeman. At the same time "Speedy" Graubart and his equally creative neighbor, Ed Schanke, pasted together a makeshift kite. They flew their creation with greater joy and pride than success. Together these three events brought sharp retribution.

Shortly thereafter the Secretariat dispatched notices to each room, asking every internee to sign the paper and to abstain from further violations of the rules. The note reported the German position that the bottle throwing had threatened local safety, that the kite flying had damaged vegetation, and that none should pick any vegetables or plants (including dandelions and other weeds). At the end Patzak made the ominous observation that any repetition of these breaches of discipline "may have unpleasant consequences for the group in general."[20] The incidents and the Germans' reaction provoked intense exchange among the Americans over the offenders' motives, the authoritarian responses, and their childish behaviour. Juvenile pranks provided a necessary emotional outlet.

With spring the calisthenics group conducted by Lattu and Lovell assumed greater importance among the internees. In part, more individuals found the higher temperatures conducive to exercise and social interaction. As part of this spring fever the internees turned to playing baseball as a further form of exercise and group activity. Kennan negotiated the use of the municipal athletic field. This facility, about a mile from the hotel, enjoyed a marvelous natural setting. Surrounded on three sides by forest and set on a high knoll, the field enjoyed a wide-sweeping view from its open side. Even for those not concerned with athletics, the park-like area provided a pleasant stroll. The Americans could use the field four times a week which provided

Everett Holt at bat

a consistent physical outlet. Lovell had brought along a regulation softball, a bat, and two gloves, which provided the equipment for league play. The participants protected them with great care. For practice, the players made their own balls of stockings, adhesive tape, and other makeshift materials with champagne corks and golf balls for centers. The resident doctors sewed them together with their surgical instruments. When struck by an equally makeshift bat created from tree limbs, the ersatz balls tended to disintegrate or assume strange shapes but served their purpose.

The group organized a four-team league - the Embassy Reds, the Embassy Blues, the Journalists, and the Army and Navy. Lattu made bases from the diplomatic mail pouches, while someone else manufactured home plate, with wooden pegs, from commissary boxes. Robert Chalker made the "Wurlitzer Cup" for the winner of the "Bad Nauheim Wurlitzer Cup Baseball Series." He made the elegant cup from an empty cracker can and engraved it with a punch. Lt. Col. Smith became the league president and rules interpreter, since no one had a rule book. Over fifty men participated, and the games drew large crowds from the hotel. The arguments over rules interpretations, eligibility, umpires' decisions, and talent distribution pushed thoughts of isolation, food, and departure aside for a few weeks. The bemused guards were more concerned about the sanity of their charges than the rules of the game. Kennan, who caught for the Embassy Reds, credited the baseball competition for shifting the Americans' concentration from their personal concerns to happier considerations during the final weeks of internment.[21]

While baseball helped offset depression, the group constantly faced the uncertainty of their status. They heard nothing directly from Washington, D.C. and learned of the German-American exchanges through interpreting Patzak's enigmatic remarks and whatever the Swiss reported to Morris and Kennan. They were plagued with a growing conviction that nobody cared, no one wanted them, and no one would help their plight. Such beliefs created a melancholic attitude which grew with time. To be sure, Bad Nauheim University, the entertainment evenings, and the BBC news of the war with Germany, provided many distractions, but each night the individual confronted his or her own private thoughts. These considerations were not always happy or pleasant. While there were no serious open clashes or disruptive actions among the internees, there were some nervous difficulties and anxiety attacks. The inadequate diet brought on a few cases of undernourishment and serious concern about exhaustion. On the whole, however, the internees did well both psychologically and physically.

The uncertainty of their status was a further challenge to many. Many of the internees had special problems: they had become expatriate Americans who loved Europe and had little desire to return home. Louis Harl had a French wife, five children, and a farm in Brittany. Joachim Weidhass had a pregnant German wife in Berlin, Elfriede Kayser had a German fiance, and others also had strong European bonds. Many were not looking forward to seeing their country again.

Charles O'Neil and Major John Lovell

Unquestionably, the most seriously affected was the reporter, Robert Best. After service with the American Expeditionary Force in the First World War, he had returned to Europe in 1923. A large man, with high-laced boots and a big hat, he had become a fixture in the Cafe Louvre in Vienna. Best welcomed most of the European journalists whenever they came to that city. He became a fine story teller and enjoyed his reputation for eccentricity, not a unique trait among the journalists of the time. In 1941 he did not show any mental problems but he could not find an answer to the dilemma of whether to return to America and an entirely new world or to renounce his country and return to his beloved Vienna. [22]

On March 3 he left the group for Berlin. Shortly afterward he sent a post card, addressed to the American School of Diplomats, Relief Workers, and Newspapermen, informing them of his return to Vienna. Morris took immediate exception, and wrote him a brief response, telling Best that he should not write to the members of the American mission. Best, clearly unstable, wrote a scurrilous, disoriented reply voicing anti-Semetic, anti-Roosevelt, and anti-Morris thoughts. He had slipped around a bend in the road of life and could not turn back.[23]

At the time, Best's departure disturbed only the handful of people, while the majority understood his strained loyalties. Few anticipated that he would later become a rabid mouthpiece for the Nazis. The stress impacted on everyone but it broke Best.

The only all-inclusive, constant weapon against the uncertainties of confinement at Bad Nauheim was the rumor. Throughout the internment the rumor sustained morale. Despite their specific injunction against rumors Morris and Kennan quickly adjusted their thinking on the issue. They could not stop them and rumors provided a form of therapy for people confined with uncertain hope for relief. In the first months of 1942 the internees obtained much relief through "reliable," "current," "optimistic" reports concerning their future. Morris and Kennan, whether from intent or resignation, participated in the circulation of hopeful reports.

Mineral water pump of Bad Nauheim

When the eight-person American contingent from Copenhagen arrived on January 25 (bringing the total to 137 in Bad Nauheim) they brought the first happy, news from the outside. They reported that a Swedish newspaper had published an account that a Portugese ship, the *Nyassa* (8,000 tons, built in 1905) had sailed for New York. It would bring the German internees to Lisbon on February 15 for the exchange. They speculated that the Danish government had expedited their transfer to Bad Nauheim in order to assure their departure with the main American group. Morris gave some credence to the report noting that the Portugese could use the money and that the exchange would inevitably take place in Lisbon. As time passed, however, this strongly held belief was discarded in favor of credence in a Swiss news account, asserting that an American ship would transport them. This new idea replaced the one about the *Nyassa*, which was then termed the "rotten in Denmark" ship story.

Onnie Lattu and Francis Cunningham

The American ship tale was probably the product of idle talk and strong aspiration. It did not survive long. As it passed away, a strong speculation arose that an Italian ship, *Conte Grande*, would serve as the exchange vessel. The fact that the Secretariat allowed the publication of the report in the *Pudding* gave it a greater substance for belief. But that phantom ship foundered quickly.[26] It found replacement in the notorious faux pas of the Swiss diplomat, Zuber, and the Secretariat in prematurely releasing the news that the American and German authorities were in agreement over the exchange. This information spread like wildfire, only to be doused by the confiscation of the *Pudding*. Before that story had disappeared completely, there arose another tale that the Swedish *Kungsholm* was leaving for them on March 18. This last idea came from the Central Americans.[27]

Ultimately, Morris served as the source for the report (he had it from a Swiss newspaper) that the Swedish ship *Drottningholm* had departed New York for Lisbon on March 17.[28] This happy prospect fell partial victim to a letter from Berlin to Lochner, reporting that the German.Foreign Office had confirmed the use of the ship, its guarantee of safe passage by all the belligerents—and its need for a major overhaul. If they were going home on the Drottningholm, they could not go immediately.[29]

On March 29 Morris and Kennan received confirmation that the *Drottningholm* would transfer them. They did not, however, have a date, and the Swiss suggested some caution in hoping for an early departure.[30] The internees took heart, however, that this rumor might have some truth, since Zorn and the hotel authorities began inspecting rooms for damages and presenting individual bills for payment. Such sudden bureaucratic action heralded change.

On April 23 a notice appeared on the bulletin board. It proclaimed that the *Drottningholm* had sailed from Goteborg, Sweden, with 150 Americans aboard, on April 19. It would leave New York with the German internees on May 5, arriving in Lisbon on May 14, and departing for New York with the Bad Nauheim Americans ten days later.[31] The rumors were over; they were going home.

NOTES

[1]Fischer, "Diary," 4 January 1942.

[2]He quoted the mythical faculty member, Professor Wurlitzer: "I am acquainted with all the leading educational institutions. I know of no one which excells Old Badheim University in the watchful protection it gives its students against the outer world during the formative years of their training." A copy of the prospectus is in the Lochner Papers. Whitcomb added wryly that Badheim was "the largest free American University on the continent of Europe." He could not find a teacher for the single course in the Faculty of Domestic Economy: "War-time housekeeping." Nonetheless he promised all students commencement exercises worthy of those passing "to the Unknown World that has for so long been the object both of its dreams and its preparations."

[3]*Bad Nauheim Pudding,* vol. 1 no. 2, p. 3.

[4]The Tuesday-night sports presentations were conducted by individuals who had participated in the activity during their college days. Examples were: boxing (Lovell), wrestling (Graubart), fencing (White), football (Conger), rugby (Whitcomb), baseball (Smith). The Thursday-night series concerned travel observations: Transjordania (Morris), India (Lehman), Congo (Simper), Russia (Kennan), Greek Islands (Morris), New Orleans (Oechsner), Milwaukee (Steinkopf), etc.

[5]Fischer, "Diary," 27 March. Steinkopf passed the censorship off in his remarks by suggesting that the Lochners' Scottie had inadvertently eaten portions of the program script. Smith and Lovell, "Story," Part II, p. 4.

[6]Perhaps the loudest laugh came from a remark parodying George Kennan, "You can wait for some of the people all of the time, and all of the people some of the time, BUT YOU CAN'T WAIT FOR ALL OF THE PEOPLE ALL OF THE TIME." Copies of most of the presentations are in the Lochner Papers. Other thoughts are in Fischer, "Notes," pp. 48, 52; "Diary," 6 February, 28 March, Kennan, "Report" pp. 37-38; White, "Diary," 29 March; Lattu Interview. Herman's diary suggests friction between Whitcomb and the Secretariat. On 2 March 1942 Whitcomb resigned but reconsidered under persuasion. Herman, "Diary," 2 March 1942.

[7]Kennan, "Report," p. 37; Smith and Lovell, "Story," Part II, p. 7. Debate was also a form of entertainment. In March the diplomats and journalists debated "Resolved, diplomats have been a greater nuisance in the world than journalists." Each side had to castigate itself. The journalists won. Herman, "Diary," 11 March 1942.

[8]A marvelous exchange took place between the assistant editors Thuermer and Conger who were competing with each other for the attention of the Lochner daughter, Rosemarie. As they were mimeographing the first issue, Thuermer remarked, "I am doing this to save my face." Conger quickly retorted, "Why save it?" Fischer, "Diary," 6 February.

[9]The front page clearly contravened Morris' published injunction against spreading rumors. Morris and Kennan obviously had some uncertainty allowing rumors to circulate officially. The issue of February 7 sank the rumor of a Portugese ship, the *Nyassa*, taking them home. The story ended, "In view of what happened to the *Nyassa* story, no use getting all steamed up over rumors."

[10]The basic story is in Fischer "Diary," 3 March. The situation of an American publication in an American community being confiscated by American authorities created more than a little concern. White, "Diary," 7 March, 1942.

[11]Interestingly, the principals, Kennan and Lochner, made no mention of the problem in their subsequent writings. The correspondents, who had contended with the vagaries of Nazi censorship, viewed the *Pudding* as a labor of love and shed no tears over its demise. Four issues were enough. Grambling, *Free Men are Fighting*, pp. 387-388. On the occasion of their Washington D.C. reunion in February 1981, the survivors brought out volume II, no. 1 of the *Pudding* with an updated list of the internees and updated biographies of many survivors.

[12]Lochner, *What About Germany*?, p. 370. Herman's diary provides some meaningful comment on the food problem.

[13]Kennan, "Report," pp. 24-25; Smith and Lovell, "Story," Part II, p. 4. The diaries of White, Fischer, and Herman provide a continuous litany of complaint over the food issue. Thomas Bailey had brought along a scale, which he made available to the group in Lovell's room. Honenthal carefully made a chart, detailing the military height and weight ratios. While some people actively dieted because of the supportive environment, the majority found the prospect maddening. In the end, the average weight loss for men was ten pounds; for women, 6.7 pounds. Smith and Lovell, "Story," Part II, p. 10. Lochner, *What About Germany*? p. 371. Most of the internees kept track of their weight; some, like Commander White, maintained a compulsive daily record.

[14]White "Diary," 23 January, 1942; Kennan, "Report," p. 22.

[15]The first issue of the *Pudding* carried a piece, "Fags Failing, Butte Boom," which included, "Three types of snipe-hunters were reported operating: the furtive who flick their cigarette butts into their packets until they can open them privately or who move to a quiet corner with an ashtray and empty it into an envelope; the bold who fill their pipe above board after openly snaring and breaking open a butt; the hygenic who carefully snip off the lip-sticked stub with a scissors or pen-knife. It went on that the diplomats left the most desirable butts, while those at the newsmen's tables were not worth gathering. The Bad Nauheim Pudding, vol. 1, no 1, 7 February, 1942, p. 5. The most successful butt hunter was the newsman from Vienna, Robert Best. Fischer, "Notes," p. 47.

[16]Louis P. Lochner, *Always the Unexpected*, pp. 275-276. Fischer "Diary," 22 March, Fischer, "Notes," p. 56; Smith and Lovell, "Story," Part II, p. 11. Some topers chose trickery since bribary was expensive. Three happy souls enjoyed a glorious game in which one would engage the guard in loud argument while another filched the winemaster's keys and removed a bottle or two. The third person watched carefully and disposed of the subsequent empty bottles. Interview with Dagfin Hoynes, October 1985.

[17]In the most suspicious case a married journalist and a divorcee established a more serious relationship. One of the observers recalled that in one of the parlor games, the offending male was listed as a jockey for a horse, "Indiscretion - by Hearsay out of Cognac." Fischer, "Diary," 9 January.

[18]Fischer, "Notes," p. 51, story by Ernest Fischer in the Lochner papers.

[19]Smith and Lovell, "Story," Part II, p. 6, Fischer, "Notes," p. 39. Some of the non-participants took satisfaction in noting the prompt removal of Hitler's large picture from the lobby wall. They credited the fear of another throwing incident for the removal. Fischer, "Diary," 9 March. Commander White wrote a poem, "Ode to an urn" which ended:

A plaintive tune sings each
spitoon
Henceforth on Badheim floors:
I'd rather be a chamber pot
And live behind closed doors.

[20]A copy is in the Lochner papers. White, "Diary," 29 April, 1942. Fischer, "Diary," 29 April; Graubart interview. The latter's good spirits and prankster attitude toward the entire affair constantly put him in mild, but never serious, jeopardy. When the Gestapo permitted the first extensive walks he carefully learned the pace of the older guards. Then, together with Lattu and Lovell, he chose a day for a blistering pace going away from the hotel. As the tired group started home no one noticed the time. When the punctilious guards finally noted that they would be tardy in reaching the hotel, they forced everyone into a doubletime pace, to the delight of the three perpetrators. Ibid.

[21]Kennan, "Report," pp. 28-29; Smith and Lovell, "Story," Part I, p. 12; Ibid, Part Ii, p. 8; White "Diary," 16 April, 1942. The Embassy Reds were the champions.

[22]The White "Diary" provides an insightful study of his deterioration under confinement. This poetry also explained his growing anger over their condition and frustrated bafflement over doing anything about it. A strong willed-man, he understood his problem, but his awarenss only added to it. See also Grambling, *Free Men are Fighting*, pp. 387-389.

[23]Copies of the exchange are in the Lochner papers. Most people clearly accepted Best's departure without undue rancor. For the sad conclusion of Best's activities (he became a twisted speaker for the Nazis, employing the nom de plume, "Guess Who") see Nathaniel Weyl, *Treason: The Story of Disloyalty and Betrayal in American History* (Washington, D.C.: Public Affairs Press, 1950) pp. 363-366; Margaret Boveri, *Treason in the Twentieth Century* trans. by Jonathan Steinberg (London: MacDonald, 1961), pp. 177-179. William L. Shirer described Best's story in fictionalized form in *The Traitor* (New York: Farrar, Straus, 1950) and in "The American Radio Traitors."

[24]White, "Diary," 25, 26 January 1942; Fischer, "Diary," 25 January. The proposal gained greater support when a newsman received a letter, suggesting the same news, from a German colleague. *Ibid*, 27 January. Other reports, seemingly substantiating the dream, came from sources in Germany and Hungary.

[25]*Bad Neuheim Pudding*, 7 February, 1942, p. 1.

[26]Ibid, 14 February 1942, p. 1. A disenchanted White put his feelings into words: "It would probably be sounder to allow oneself no hopes of any kind. After all the only solution to troubles is death—preferably a quick and painless one, suffered in the performance of some action which one believes to be worthy." White, "Diary," 27 February, 1942.

[27]White, "Diary," 15 March 1942. As part of the rumor mill, Sam Woods, the commercial attache, carefully informed Ernest Fischer that they would definitely leave on March 26. Under further interrogation, Woods indicated that he had the facts from a friend who had them from the wife of a foreign office representative at a Berlin party. Fischer, "Diary," 14 March.

[28]Ibid, 19 March. George Kennan proposes that he received the news from the Swiss legation in Berlin. As well, he proposes that the internees knew of it before he could announce the news. Kennan, "Story," p. 24.

[29]Ibid, 22 March; White, "Diary," 22 March 1942. The Drottningholm was built at Stephen and Sons in Glasgow in 1905 as one of the first turbine vessels in the world. She joined the Swedish American Line in 1920 and ferried passengers around the world. During the Second World War she transfered many internees. Letter from Borje Nygren, Krigsarkivet, 16 July 1985.

[30]The Germans accepted the principle of the exchange on 21 March, when they communicated the understanding to the Swiss, who forwarded everything to Washington D.C. Harrison (Bern) to Secretary of State, 26 March, 1942. File 701.6211/1635. A general review of the entire transfer of internees is in Arnold M. Krammar, "In Splendid Isolation: Enemy Diplomats in World War II," *Prologue*, 17 (Spring 1985), pp. 25-43.

[31]Fischer "Diary," 23 April.

CHAPTER V

GOING HOME

For we're not out until we're out
Let none of you forget it
A date just doesn't mean a thing
Unless the Germans set it.
Warning to Optimists

The announcement of their certain departure promptly improved everyone's attitude. From the growing disgruntlement of uncertainty, the pettiness of boredom, the languor of involuntary confinement metamorphosed a regenerated spirit of hope and direction. Clearly everyone's reactions varied as did his or her obligations and responsibilities. Everyone cleared up his or her affairs, began the tedium of packing one's belongings (despite their difficulties, many remembered the proverbial idea that three moves equaled one fire), and discarded their immediate concerns about internment in favor of planning the future. Life assumed an acceptable rhythm once more.[1]

For some, the proximity of release created a sense of panic over neglected promises and intentions. This concern was most evident among the journalists and the military attaché personnel. The former made their living with words in competition with each other and remained, as a result, more isolated than their military colleagues. In January Lochner, anticipating future release, had called a conference of the newsmen, and had raised the issue of writing a collective book, with each colleague contributing a chapter of 5,000 words. Oechsner responded that he and his UP staff would not have time for such an enterprise and agreed with Lochner that any publication would require approval from their respective agencies. At a subsequent meeting, four UP men—Oechsner, Grigg, Fleischer, and Conger—excused themselves, pleading the uncertain pressure from their New York office as their excuse.[2]

Thereafter, various individuals worked intermittently on their contributions to some collective effort. While they were interned together, they could not overlook the individual nature of their trade nor the intense competition driving them. All of the correspondents knew that the story of Bad Neuheim would bring recognition and columns of newsprint. Freed from the lassitude of Berlin and the interminable struggle with the Nazi censors, they could, in their own free world, make a reputation for themselves. Or, more precisely, the initial reports would gain glory and recognition; the tardy would obtain a comparatively negative reward. Therefore most of the journalists scribbled their notes in preparation for release, and the April 23 announcement spurred them to intense competition.[3]

The military attachés, particularly the army group, under Lovell's direction, also put down their observations and ideas. They accepted his prediction that the War Department would expect such reports because they possessed some collective insights from their German internment. With the onset of war, Lovell argued, the Army lacked basic knowledge concerning Germany and Hitler's Reich. He possessed the intellectual persuasiveness of his craft which won him support from his colleagues. Each member of his selected group drew up his individual written report without one person knowing about the other's contribution. Lovell assumed full responsibility for smuggling the reports past any German inspection.[4]

For the majority of the internees, survival was of more vital interest than providing a chronicle. The increasing British air raids on Frankfurt provided much food for uneasy thought. The more pessimistic worried that some misguided British bombers might drop their explosives prematurely on the Grand Hotel as a final irony. Throughout their stay the British air force had mounted numerous bombing attacks on Frankfurt. The concerned internees could plainly observe the German anti-aircraft defenses in action around the large city and, on occasion, could see the bombardment of Stuttgart. British bombers often passed over the hotel approaching their objective or en route home. Occasionally the military attaches observed aircraft shot down. They had numerous active reminders that the war was around them but, as non-participants, had no chance to take action.[5] Only when repatriation loomed larger in their consciousness did the majority suddenly consider the fortunes of war worthy of note.

Complicating these fears was the loss of rumor as a collective means of relieving the stress of confinement. Now the internees confronted a realized dream, without any outlet for the resultant strain. The prospect of release dissolved the spiritual cement keeping the group together, maintaining discipline and order. The departure date became the focal point, as a dividing moment between the collective past experience and the individual, uncertain, future.[6] Relief brought reality.

Added to the sudden collective awareness of self as opposed to the group's welfare was the first direct communication from Washington. The Department of State had continued negotiating with the Germans through the Swiss but had found no reason for direct contact with their lonely representatives in Bad Nauheim. As Kennan and Morris prepared for their return, their superiors in Washington, D.C. suddenly took notice. They informed the interned diplomats of the Controller General's Office's preliminary ruling that, since many of them were temporary or short-term employees and had not been working, they would not be paid for their time in Bad Nauheim! They could count on payment through December 14, 1941 but not thereafter.

Other issues which interested the State Department, to Kennan's chagrin, were the possibility of holding some German diplomats for a second voyage of the *Drottningholm* and of repatriating only half of the Americans this trip, in favor of giving the space to refugees. The authorities worked matters out, but in the process they created more than a little stress and anger among the diplomats stranded in Germany.[7]

The euphoria associated with leaving their cramped luxury accommodations, the arrival of various commissary goods purchased through the Swiss, and a dramatic improvement in the hotel meals helped maintain a certain tranquility. On May 5 Patzak announced that the group would depart Bad Nauheim at 10:26 p.m. on May 12. The internees spent the intervening week in winding up their affairs (some people had run up some large bills, as much as $800) and organizing the responsibilities and assignments for departure. Once more, the attachés, working under Kennan's guidance, organized a military structure with direct lines of control. Each car would have a commander with three subordinates (a deputy commander, an adjutant, and a runner) with company designations beneath them. Each company had given letter designations—had a commander who was in charge of three to five people. Each commander had specific orders which forbade anyone leaving the train, conversing with Germans unless absolutely necessary, changing sleeping assignments, or wandering independently through the train.[8]

The instructions did not mean much to two members of the group. Felix Pflicht, who was married to a pregnant member of the Embassy staff, learned that he must wait for a subsequent sailing of the *Drottningholm*. More serious was the plight of Werner John, born of a divorced American mother and German father, who discovered that his mother and sister could leave but that the German authorities wanted him for military service.[9] Sad scenes followed this news, since many people understood that those left behind might not see the United States again. Individuals caught up in the international macrocosm could not control their fate.[10]

May 12 was "Der Tag." As could be expected the anticipation created much excitement but also allowed a new focal point for complaint. Since the train would have only a single first-class and one second-class car, the others being third-class, many people registered vigorous protests over the travel arrangements. While the Germans promised two dining cars, which was certain to make life easier than the Berlin-Bad Nauheim trip, few people paid any attention to that fact. Earlier, fear and uncertainty had made the train assignments bearable; now, with the return of status, and awareness of the homeward journey, they suddenly remembered earlier complaints (the chief suspicion being that the Embassy officials had privately enjoyed a much higher standard of living than the non-diplomats), and petty individual grievances made people more vocal. Obviously Kennan's job was not an easy one, since he confronted all of the emotional upset of impatient internees on the point of release while organizing the departure. Newsreel photographers invaded the hotel for the departure and disturbed the efforts of many people to quietly enjoy their final day in Bad Nauheim.

Departure from Bad Nauheim

At 8:00 p.m., following a happy meal of duck (whereby the Germans sought to impress the departing Americans but made many of them ill) when most people put aside their grievances, if only temporarily, in favor of the feverish gaity which is the hallmark of such occasions, the group assembled in the hotel lobby. They walked the mile to the train station, arriving with only minutes to spare for a new departure time at 9:26 p.m. Patzak, as a measure of courtesy, allowed them to walk the distance without escort. The group presented an interesting sight for the few Germans watching their departure. Expecting an early repatriation, many of the internees had given most of their wardrobes to German friends in December. After five months many people wore clothing which had clearly seen better days. On the other hand, some individuals had saved their best clothing for the departure day. The contrast between the threadbare, patched dress of some in contrast to the elegance of others created a difference begging description.

The train left at 9:25 p.m. among much shouting and general enthusiasm that they were going home. The military attachés exclaimed, with pointed double meaning, "So long, we'll be back." When asked about returning, "Speedy" Graubart, responded acidly, "Only to sow it with salt."[11] Their less reverent journalist colleagues sang their own refrain (to the tune of "It's a Long, Long Trail"):

> I want to go home on the Drottningholm
> Where unemployed diplomats play
> Where seldom is heard
> An intelligent word
> And the bar stays open night and day.[12]

"All aboard"

The train crept through Frankfurt a half hour later, with mixed group reactions. Some made derisive remarks about the home of the pudding manufacturers, while others prayed silently that the Allies would not bomb the city that night. Once out of the urban area, the train hurried toward France. The frenetic excitement drained most of the internees who, despite cramped quarters and earlier complaints, slipped off to sleep earlier than usual.

They awakened the next morning in France. The train moved around Paris at noon on a belt-line railway before reaching the line Orleans, Tours, Bourdeaux. Incidents along the way gave them conversational topics. Just south of Paris someone tossed a rock at the train, smashing a window in the dining car and showering glass shards on Oechser and Joe Grigg, who were enjoying their soup. Whether an accident or a political statement, the incident kept people from the windows for a few hours. A little south of that point, a peasant working in the field suddenly unfurled an American flag which he waved wildly at the passing train. His action impressed everyone, both for his courage and for the intelligence network that must have told him who was on the train. Along the way the journalists tossed cigarettes on station platforms whenever the train slowed or stopped briefly. They enjoyed the joyous excitement of the French, who "dived for the smokes as if they were pearls."[13]

The group awakened the next morning in Biarritz. The Germans, after some confusion about whether to leave their charges on the train or to put them into a hotel, loaded everyone on busses and moved them to the Hotel du Palais, which had once been the site of a palace belonging to Napoleon III, but which had fallen on less prosperous times. The Germans carefully assigned the Americans to specific rooms while maintaining full control with numerous guards. Since the train lacked any facilities for bathing, everyone had a warm bath before thinking about other matters. Some wandered into the bar, where they encountered the Central American diplomats from Bad Nauheim, who had arrived on another train. This contact was the first the Americans had had in five months with non-Germans.[14] Subsequently the Germans allowed a long, escorted stroll along the beach. The noteworthy problem was the execrable food (rated "double X lousy" by one), which was worse than that in Bad Nauheim and the dilapidated state of the city, which evidenced neglect under the ravages of war.

While the Germans kept the group under watch, with a 9:00 p.m. curfew, they missed several people who wanted to see the city by night. Lattu, Fischer, and two or three others eluded their guards and spent the night on the town. When the French discovered their nationality, many of them gave messages for American relatives and friends. Lattu had the greatest success, since he obtained some addresses and invitations from the local women before returning to the hotel.[15] Fleischer spent the night moving from bar to bar before he returned, slightly the worse for his activities, to the hotel, and the expected angry remarks. He was not in any condition to really care and reported that he had observed many signs, "Speaking English is Prohibited," which he had rejected in favor of accepting local hospitality.[16]

At 6:00 a.m. the next morning heavy gunfire awakened everyone. The hotel shook with the impact of the noise. At first most people thought that the allies were bombing the city. After they discovered the reality nearly everyone watched the sham German landing exercise. The realism frightened a good many as they observed a battalion-size training exercise with much noise and smoke. Whether the activity had been scheduled without thought of the Americans or planned as an impressive reminder of German prowess remained a mystery. Still, the attaches took notes, while others cowered under their beds.[17]

At 10:00 a.m. the Germans put their charges on the train again for the last leg of the trip—to Hendaye where the internees moved across a train platform to Spanish trains. The Gestapo guards departed, leaving only a few foreign office representatives as a reminder of German presence. Kennan had to divide his flock among two trains; the women and officers receiving sleepers, while the others used day cars. Morris assumed control of the first train, with only Americans while Kennan had the second with Americans and the Central Americans. While the cars were crowded, the meals—soup, fish, meat, etc.—were the best many of them had enjoyed in two years.[18]

Complaints were few. The news organizations, AP and UP, sent wine and liquor aboard for the journalists, who shared their bounty with their compatriots. In addition to these spirits, many individuals purchased Spanish cognac at every stop. The celebration grew more raucous as people drank more than was good for them in wild happiness over their release. This excess created much difficulty for the train leaders, since they halted for five hours at Camp del Medina (apparently at German insistence until the latter knew the *Drottningholm's* location). Morris and Kennan locked the doors of the trains in an effort to keep the Americans aboard. But they achieved only limited success, as some of the former internees climbed out the windows and carried on with their loud revelries. The combination of Spanish cognac and freedom resulted in a highly independent and unruly attitude. The car commanders finally assembled all their charges—having physically boosted some of them back on the train—and reported their presence as the trains departed around 2:00 a.m.

They reached the Spanish-Portugese border at a mountain station, Vilar Formoso, about 9:00 a.m., where Ted Rousseau, the assistant naval attaché in Lisbon, met them. Kennan conferred with Rousseau about various practical matters and then asked for breakfast. After five months of dealing with endless complaints concerning food, space, people, and every other conceivable problem, Kennan extracted a small measure of revenge. He gorged himself with a huge breakfast, while his bedraggled charges nursed the results of their wild excesses. After completing his meal, a satisfied Kennan permitted the train to continue on for Lisbon. To pass the time he turned to poetry, composing a farewell poem for his companions:

From you, embattled comrades in abstention,
Compatriots to this or that degree,
Who've shared with me the hardships of detention
In Jeschke's Grand and guarded hostelry—

From you, my doughty champions of the larder,
Who've fought with such persistency and skill,
Such mighty hearts, such overwhelming ardor,
The uninspiring battle of the swill—

From you, my friends, from your aggrieved digestions,
From all the pangs of which you love to tell,
Your dwindling flesh and your enraged intestines:
Permit me now to take a fond farewell.

For five long months, you've slept and nursed your bellies,
Or strolled along the Usa's quiet shores,
Eaten your rolls and failed to eat your jellies,
While others toiled and tramped and fought the wars.

The world might choke in food-restricting measures;
Chinese might starve, and Poles might waste away;
But God forbid that you—my tender treasures—
Should face the horrors of a meatless day.[19]

Berlin
Bad Nauheim
Biarritz
Lisbon

The trains reached Lisbon about two hours apart (7:30 and 9:30 p.m.). The platform was, in both cases, a mob scene, without anyone in control. While members of the American Embassy and Consulate were present with hotel assignments, they could not control the mass confusion which quickly destroyed all pretense of order. Many of the internees boosted their suitcases out of the windows to Portugese porters, who had no idea which buses to put the baggage on. After some intense haggling over who and what were going where, the individuals sorted themselves out and shifted to hotels in Sentra and Estorial (resorts just outside Lisbon). As they boarded their buses a curious German, just off the *Drottningholm*, remarked to Steinkopf that the United States was going downhill "Its a place where you can't get cuffs with pants." An enraged Steinkopf, fully aware of his own shabby clothes, retorted, "In Germany, a citizen not only cannot get cuffs with his pants, he can't get pants."[20]

. . . on the dock at Alcantara Wharf, Lisbon

With their departure from the trains, the ex-internees were once more at liberty, and Kennan and Morris were no longer responsible for them.[21] The two had successfully carried out the internment without major upheaval or serious friction. The 132 individuals whom they had guided from Bad Nauheim to Lisbon were now free.[22] The Americans could move about, buy newspapers, and eat (most of them quickly suffered illness from over-eating) what they wanted in peace. For the first time in five months of incarceration, they were free of the armed Gestapo guards, the blackout precautions, the problems of wartime Germany, and the restrictive demands of their own diplomatic leaders.

The majority spent their first free hours sending messages to loved ones, announcing their safe arrival in Lisbon. Some found cablegrams awaiting them, which brought solace after five months of silence. As they sat down to a late meal in Portugal most were happy over reaching safety. For the newsmen, however, the dinner did not last long. En route Oechsner and Lochner had agreed not to send off a lot of copy (a partial explanation was Morris's threat to keep the journalists incommunicado until the *Drottningholm* sailed), but telegrams from their New York offices, demanding stories, destroyed the flimsy truce. Both sides broke it without informing the other about the betrayal. The re-entry into the reality of their competitive world did not allow much pause for reflection or breath. Those newsmen lodged in Estorial hired taxicabs for the one-hour ride back to Lisbon and stayed up most of the night filing their stories. They did so well that the Portugese censors broke down under the language problems. On May 18 the censors refused any more English-language transmissions. The journalists could relax and join the others in enjoying their freedom.

SS Drottningholm, Lisbon

On May 22 the Americans could board the *Drottningholm*. As agreed upon between the belligerents, she was painted white with the large dark letters, DIPLOMAT, on both sides of the hull. For some, the day confirmed the end of frivolous flirtation (some legitimate mates appeared to disrupt relationships, some individuals turned to new assignments, some simply stayed in Portugal, and some agreed to continue the relationship); for others, it terminated a major period in their lives, and some found the stress unbearable. One of these was Louis Harl, who had come aboard with all of his baggage. As the whistle heralded departure, he announced to Thuermer one of his compartment colleagues, "I'm going to stay with my wife and children." He walked out and down the gangplank, leaving his baggage without thought. Another such was Joachim Weidhass, who started back for Berlin and his wife.

Many of the group—military attachés, journalists, and diplomats—had other assignments and therefore did not sail for home. Although life had remained still for five months, the return of normal requirements pushed members of the group in all directions. Some of the diplomats discovered the gratitude of their government when they found orders assigning them to posts in Portugal. They were to report for work the next day.

"Bon Voyage"
from those left behind in Lisbon

Aboard ship the internees quickly merged into a different world. The 875 passengers included Admiral William D. Leahy, returning from his service as Ambassador to Vichy France with the body of his deceased wife; the American Ambassador to Hungary, Herbert Pell; and numerous other American diplomatic representatives. With them were many fortunate European refugees. One could walk the deck for long periods of time without hearing any English.[24] The ship was a floating Tower of Babel, but one with the heady delights of freedom. Blessedly the *Drottningholm* suffered no rationing problems.

Captain of the SS Drottningholm

. . . on the way home

The trip progressed without memorable incident, and the ship entered New York harbor on May 30.[25] Life on the *Drottningholm* had been akin to living on a prolonged trolley trip. It provided an anti-climax in getting them across the water. They were headed home! Lower Manhattan was blacked out and searchlights traced curious paths across the sky. While the city's superficial appearance was not much different than Berlin in December, 1941, the passengers, including the many internees, knew the difference. As their pastor noted, "All of us needed new clothes, an alphabet or two of vitamins, and a deep draught of fresh American air."[26]

TIME
THE WEEKLY NEWSMAGAZINE

THE PRESS

Back from the Axis

At Lisbon the sweating Portuguese censors begged for mercy. Aboard the Swedish liner *Drottningholm*, the third-class bar shook and trembled with the chattering of typewriters. In Manhattan last week the fountains of prose still poured out, orally and in print. Twenty-two word-congested correspondents who for five months of Axis internment had not been able to file a dispatch were finally satisfying their urge, telling of loot, mayhem and starvation in occupied countries, of Axis morale that has begun to sag in Germany, is almost finished in Italy but still does not warrant easy optimism in the U.S.

Some of their tales of their own five months in limbo:

Ersatz Reciprocity. Nazi treatment of interned correspondents was allegedly keyed to treatment of Axis correspondents and diplomats in the U.S. Arrested after midnight, most of them had a sinking premonition that they were due to spend the rest of the war in a Gestapo prison. An exception was I.N.S. Correspondent Hugo Speck. Alcoholically fortified, he sprawled on the floor at Alexanderplatz prison, went to sleep while 18 other correspondents waited tensely in a large detention room. Awaking to a guard's prodding, he heaved himself upright on the guard's arm, shouting "Hello, buddy."

Soon transferred along with U.S. diplomats to Bad Nauheim Spa, the correspondents renamed their hotel the "Grand Refrigerator." Its guests ate dumplings and sauerkraut three times a week and were bullied in minor ways by Gestapo men. To fight boredom the internees set up "Badheim University" (Motto: "Education of the ignorant by the ignorant"), offered a curriculum of drama (U.P.'s Fred Oechsner), Shakespeare & Phonetics (Chicago *Tribune's* Alex Small), Scientific Bridge (U.P.'s Pat Conger), with miscellaneous courses ranging from tap dancing to philosophy and languages.

Only one correspondent among them enjoyed special privileges. He was U.P.'s Vienna stringman Robert Best, a South Carolinian and World War I artilleryman who hated Jews and Roosevelt. After March 2 the others discovered why he was favored: he was released to become another Lord Haw-Haw on the Nazi short wave. He took the Nazi name of "Mr. Guess Who."

1981 reunion
The Ladies of the Chorus
Gladys Spicknall (Anderson)
Helga Hoynes (John)
Ursula Forbes (Nett)
Ilse Heath (Herter)

1981
Captain Graubart
The Reverend Herman
Philip Fahrenholz
Ambassador George Kennan
Robert Reams, Jr.

NOTES

[1]The news changed Ernest Fischer's plans. He and Alvin Steinkopf had decided that the prospect of long internment was not for them. They planned an escape. Fischer decided on June 19—Negro Emancipation Day in Texas. The two men assiduously collected maps, put aside a few cans of food, and saved their ration coupons. They planned their movements with military precision. After climbing down the hotel's ivy exterior, they would steal around the guards (whose movements they timed systematically) and catch a freight train (they had a schedule from a maid) passing through Bad Nauheim. The Swiss border was 150 miles away. They understood the probable price of capture, but thought the risk more acceptable than the certain insanity of long-term internment. Fischer, "Notes," pp. 60-61. For a moment they considered swimming the Rhine and asked some colleagues about that waterway, indicating that the river had some "bad eddies." Their colleague, Ed Haffel, promptly responded "Not this Eddie." The prospect of returning home "on the cushion" halted the escape plans. Ibid; Fischer, "Diary," 20 April, Grambling, *Free Men are Fighting,* p. 389. Gene Graffis played solitaire night after night, betting against himself at one cent per point. When news of their relocation arrived he exclaimed "I can't leave now—I owe myself $3,193.17!" Fischer, news copy, in Lochner papers.

[2]Fischer, "Diary," 2, 4 January.

[3]For all of their tenuous agreement in Bad Nauheim, both Oechsner and Lochner clearly had their fingers crossed. Lochner's *What About Germany*? and Oechsner's (with Grigg, Fleischer, Conger, and Stadler) *This is the Enemy* (Boston: Little Brown, 1942) appeared quickly after their return home. The AP people contributed to the Oscar Grambling account, *Free Men are Fighting*. In their writing most of the participants decided against keeping their notes and burned them or flushed them down the toilet.

[4]Smith and Lovell, "Story," Part II, p. 15, Letter from Angus Thuermer, 14 August 1980. When they left Germany, Lovell had the materials carefully taped to his skin.

[5]Smith and Lovell, "Story," Part II, p. 9; Fischer, "Diary," p. 5. Not everyone followed the air war. The circumstances were different for different people. An example was the British air raid of April 1, when the attackers pounded Frankfurt with the usual din accompanying a significant air raid. That same night some people enjoyed a gloriously noisy party at Bad Nauheim into the early hours. The next morning no one mentioned the air raid, but many complained about "those drunken newsmen keeping us awake." Fischer, "Goofy Story" in Lochner Papers.

[6]White, "Diary," 2 May 1942.

[7] Harrison (Bern) to Secretary of State, 29 April 1942. File 125.0062/467; Harrison (Bern) to Secretary of State, 2 May 1942. File 701.0010/126; State Department to American Legation, Bern, 5 May 1942. File 701.0010/126. Morris had earlier protested the uncertainties of the reports concerning the group's evacuation, which made "this period very critical in holding together morale of this group, all jammed together pell mell on top of one another day and night in one hotel." See Harrison (Bern) to Secretary of State, 4 April 1942. File 703.5462/26, p. 4. Kennan, in his *Memoirs*, pp. 139-140, is particularly bitter about the neglect by his own government. The argument about wages and status went on long after the internees reached home.

[8]Directions are in Fischer, "Diary," 11 May. Fischer noted the irony of some German youngsters singing, "Weit ist der Weg in die Heimat" (it's a long way home). Ibid, 7 May. White, too, was moved by the arrival of spring and the serenity of the countryside. "There seem to be more song birds than at home, and they make a most pleasant noise. The hill outside my window is covered with green, and the Bismarcks tower on the top is half concealed. On the other side of the hotel, the medieval tower of the town of Freiburg is outlined against a peaceful sky. I wonder what awaits us." White, "Diary," 10 May 1942. An incongruous reminder of war was the arrival of silver cigarette case souvenirs for the attaches from their Berlin colleagues. Smith and Lovell, "Story," Part I, p. 15. These silver cases had the engraved signatures of the foreign attaches and were prized possessions.

[9]Fischer, "Diary," 2, 7 May; Kennan, "Report," Appendix I. Pflicht did reach America on a subsequent voyage. John served in the German army on the eastern front. Subsequently he emigrated to the United States and sought American citizenship. With his application he was drafted into the American army where he could also wear his German military decorations. Fate creates strange circumstances. Interviews with Werner John, October 1985. *The Bad Nauheim Pudding*, vol II, no. 1, February 1981; letter from Onnie Lattu, 25 January 1985.

[10]Graubart and Lattu interviews.

[11]Smith and Lovell, "Story," Part I, p. 16; Laukhuff, "Memoirs," p. 37.

[12]Fischer, "Notes," pp. 65-66; Herman, "Diary," 12 May 1942.

[13]Fischer, "Diary," 13 May; Herman, "Diary," 15, 16 May 1942, Kennan, "Report," p. 43; Lattu interview. At one stop a Frenchman crept up to the train in the dark and shared his observations on occupied France. Smith and Lovell, "Story," Part I, p. 16.

[14]Smith and Lovell, "Story," Part I, p. 16. Some of the group enjoyed this opportunity and celebrated in style. As one highly lubricated diplomat remarked, "I've been oiling the South American Axis." Fischer, "Diary," 14 May.

[15]Lattu, "Talk," p. 12; Lattu interview. He discovered the reason for the sad image of the city, i.e., the Germans had taken everything and left very little for the natives or for their own occupying troops. The hotel was in good repair but offered little else. The dining room with huge windows overlooked the beach while the tables had linen table clothes and silver place settings. The meal was mule meat, dry chick peas, and poor potatoes lacked even the Nauheim pudding as desert. Nordbye, "Memories," p. 4.

[16]Fischer, "Diary," 14, 15 May. Morris was extremely upset with Fleischer's unauthorized absence and Fleischer's refusal to be concerned about his transgression. Smith and Lovell, "Story," Part I, p. 17.

[17]Ibid; Fischer, "Diary," 15 May; White "Diary," 15 May 1942. Lochner observed the practice and reflected on how long it would be until allied troops turned the practice exercise into reality. Lochner, *What About Germany?*, p. 372. Kennan also expressed the hope that his countrymen would have, "...an opportunity of repaying the commanding general for his fireworks—generously and in kind" Kennan, "Story," p. 25.

[18]They enjoyed the obvious Spanish efforts to provide them with good food. Nonetheless the more sensitive contrasted this largess with the numbers of Spaniards who besieged them at every stop with pleas for bread and cigarettes. Fischer, "Notes," p. 67.

[19]Kennan, *Memoirs*, p. 138.

[20]Newspaper note in the Lochner Papers. For a more sobering observation concerning the German experience see Boveri, *Verzweigungen*, p. 401.

[21]Kennan, "Report," p. 45. The local American diplomatic representation had prepared a handout for them. It provided news about the harsh realities of their world. The travelers would pay for their own rooms and would not be permitted any change of rooms. Those individuals not traveling at government expense would pay $321 before obtaining passage. Interestingly, all cabins sold at the same price. The destitute could solicit funds from the Consulate office, "...provided that every reasonable effort had been made to arrange payment otherwise." At the same time, the travelers learned that they must prove that any sum beyond $250 was "not obtained in anyway benefiting the Axis countries. Copies of the injunctions are in the Lochner Papers."

[22]Five individuals from Bad Nauheim were not with them. Miss Hertha Dehmel had returned to Berlin on 28 January to take care of her aged parents; Mrs. Eleanor Hinkle had flown home on 1 April because of her advanced pregnancy; Robert Best had left on 2 March, and the Germans had detained Pflict and John in May. Herbert Burgman had not joined the group.

[23]The Lochner Papers have copies of the AP directives as well as many of the staff stories. They provide some insight into the excitement of the moment. See also Fischer, "Diary," 17, 18 May.

[24]Fisher, "Notes," p. 68; Kennan, *Memoirs*, p. 139. Morris was not one of those who spent much time on deck. As the recipient of Germany's declaration of war he carefully guarded the document against the spies, rumored to be on board. Nordbye, "Memories," pp 6-7.

[25]The Lochner Papers contain numerous accounts of the return, together with many photographs.

[26]Steward Herman, "Interfraternity Banquet at Bad Nauheim." Lattu had greater difficulties. As he helped carry the suitcases of a girlfriend from South America off the ship he spied a former girlfriend on the dock. He quickly gave the lady her baggage and landed to a joyous reception. When he asked how the lady had passed through the barriers, she quietly answered, "I told them that we would be married today." An astonished Lattu required two years for decision but did honor her presumptuous temerity. Lattu interview, October 1985.

1981
Werner John, Dagfin Hoynes, author, Onnie Lattu

BIBLIOGRAPHY

A. UNPUBLISHED RECORDS

1. National Archives, Washington, D.C. United States, Department of State, files 124.62, 125.0062, 701.0010, 701.6211, 703.5462.

   United States, State Department, file Life m 83/550.

2. *Diaries*

   Fischer, Ernest
   Hermann, Stewart W., Jr.
   Alvin J. Steinkopf
   White, Henry J.

3. *Letters*

Allard, Dean,	no date (1985)
Boyd, Carl,	September, 1984
Cunningham, Francis	October, 1985
Fischer, Ernest	October, 1980
Gauge, O,	November, 1980, August, 1984
Hennessy, Mrs. Harold	September, 1980
Keipert, Dr. Maria,	February, 1981
Kennan, George,	January, 1979, January 1985
Lovell, Mrs. Jack	July, 1980
Nygren, Borje	July, 1985
Patzak, Mrs. Elfriede	October, 1984
Schnare, Robert E.	June, 1981
Stadler, Gene	August, 1980
Steinkopf, Alvin,	January, 1981
Thuermer, Angus McLean,	August, 1980, October 1985
White, Henry J. Jr.	July, 1981

4. *Unpublished Materials*

   Laukhuff, Perry, "Memoirs"
   Nordbye, Frances, "Memories"
   Smith, Harvey H. and J.R. Lovell, "The Story of the Internment, December 14, 1941 - May 12, 1942" (Mimeographed, April 20 [sic], 1942".

5. *Interviews*

Captain Arthur Graubart,	April, 1980
Dagfin Hoynes	October, 1985
Werner John	October, 1985
Vice Admiral Onnie Lattu	May, 1981, October, 1985
Robert Levinson	August, 1979
Mrs. Katherine Smith	July, 1983
Major General Arthur Vanaman	June, 1982
Mrs. Henry J. White	April, 1981

6. *Private Papers*

Ernest Fischer in State Historical Society of Wisconsin
Stewart Herman, Jr, "Interfraternity Banquet at Bad Nauheim."
George Kennan in Princeton University
Louis P. Lochner in State Historical Society of Wisconsin

7. *Master's Thesis*

Schaleben, Joy, "Louis P. Lochner: Getting the Story Out of Nazi Germany, 1933-1941." Master of Science Thesis, Journalism, University of Wisconsin, 1967.

B. PUBLISHED MATERIALS

1. *Books*

Boveri, Margaret, *Treason in the Twentieth Century*. Translated by Jonathan Steinberg (London: MacDonald, 1961).

Boveri, Margaret, *Verzweigungen; eine Autobiographie* (Munchen: R. Piper, 1977).

Domarus, Max, *Hitler-Reden und Proklamationen, 1932-1945*, vol. II, *Untergang 1939-1945*. Munchen: Suddenstscher Verlag.

Flannery, Harry W., *Assignment to Berlin*. New York: Aflred Knopf, 1942.

Friedborg, Arvid, *Behind the Steel Wall: A Swedish Journalist in Berlin,* 1941-1943. New York: Viking Press, 1942.

Friedlander, Saul, *Prelude to Downfall: Hitler and the United States, 1939-1941*. New York: Alfred Knopf, 1967.

Grambling, Oliver, *Free Men are Fighting: The Story of World War II* (New York: Farrar and Rinehart, 1942.

Hermann, Stewart W. Jr., *Its Your Souls We Want* (New York: Harper Bros., 1943)

Israel, Fred L., *The War Diary of Breckenridge Long, Selections from the Years 1939-1944* (Lincoln: University of Nebraska, 1966).

Jonas, Manfred, *The United States and Germany, a Diplomatic History*. Ithaca: Cornell University, 1984.

Kennan, George F., *Memoirs, 1925-1950* Boston: Little Brown, 1964.

Kleeman, Rita H., *Gracious Lady: The Life of Sara Delano Roosevelt* (New York: D. Appleton-Century, 1935).

Kroneck, Friedrich J. and Thomas Oppermann, *Im Dienste Deutschlands und des Rechtes. Festschrift fur Wilhelm G. Grewe zum 70. Geburtstag am l6. Optober 1981*. Baden-Baden: Nomos Verlag, 1981.

Lochner, Louis P., *Always the Unexpected; a Book of Reminiscences* (New York: Macmillan, 1956).

Lochner, Louis P., *What About Germany* (New York: Dodd, Mead, 1942).

Ludwig, Emil, *Roosevelt, a Study in Fortune and Power*. Translated by Maurice Samuel (New York: Viking Press, 1938).

Mizener, Arthur, *The Saddest Story: A Biography of Ford Maddux Ford* (New York: World Publications, 1971).

Oechsner, Fred, *et. al., This is the Enemy* (Boston: Little Brown, 1942).

Rohwer, Jurgen & Jackel, Eberhard, *Kriegswende. Dezember 1941*. Koblenz: Bernard & Graefe, 1984.

Schmidt, Paul. *Statist auf Diplomatischer Buhne, 1923-1945. Erlebnisse des Chefdolmetschers im Auswartigen Amt mit den Staatsmannern Europas*. Wien: Ullstein Verlag, 1953.

Shirer, William L., *Berlin Diary, The Journal of a Foreign Correspondent, 1934-1941*. New York: Alfred Knopf, 1941.

Shirer, William L., *The Traitor* (New York: Farrar, Straus, 1950).

Shirer, William L., *20th Century Journey; a Memoir of a Life and the Times*, vol II, *The Nightmare Years*, 1930-1940. Boston, Little, Brown, 1984.

Smith, Howard K. *Last Train from Berlin*. New York: Alfred Knopf, 1942.

Somerfeldt, Martin H., *Das Oberkommando der Wehrmacht gibt Bekannt* (Frankfurt: Westdeutsche Verlag, 1952).

Weinberg, Gerhard L., *World in the Balance. Behind the Scenes of World War II*. Hanover, N.H.: University Press of New England, 1981.

Weyl, Nathaniel, *Treason: The Story of Disloyalty and Betrayal in American History* (Washington, D.C.: Public Affairs Press, 1950).

2. *Articles*

Conger, Clinton B. (Pat), "Guest of the Gestapo," *The Quill* Vol. 30, (August 1942), pp 3-4, 14-15.

Kittridge, Tracy B, "A Military Danger. The Revelation of Secret Strategic Plans," *United States Naval Institute Proceedings*, vol. 81.

Krammar, Arnold M, "In Splendid Isolation: Enemy Diplomats in World War II," *Prologue*, 17 (Spring, 1985), pp. 25-43.

Shirer, William L, "The American Radio Traitors," *Harper's Magazine,* 187 (October, 1943), pp. 377-404.

Weinberg, Gerhard, "Hitler's Image of the United States," *American Historical Review* 69 (July, 1964): 1006-21.

Wittels, David G., "Hitler's Short Wave Rumor Factory," *The Saturday Evening Post*, vol. 215 (November 21, 1942). pp 12-13, 117-118, 122-125.

Photographic illustrations in this book are from the following collections:

THE BERLIN DOCUMENT CENTER
Photo on page 12

THE COLLECTION OF LOUIS P. LOCHNER,
courtesy of the STATE HISTORICAL SOCIETY OF WISCONSIN
Photos on pages 34 and 81

THE COLLECTION OF ONNIE LATTU
Photos on pages 1, 4, 5, 6, 16, 19, 21, 33, 34, 40, 46, 49, 60, 72, 79, 80, 82, 83, 86, 93, 98, 99, 104, 105, and 106

THE COLLECTION OF DAGFIN HOYNES
Photos on pages 8, 10, 20, 25, 27, 35, 37, 38, 41, 43, 45, 48, 51, 52, 53, 58, 59, 60, 61, 63, 68, 73, 77, 78, 82, 84, 87, 107, 108, 110, 113

THE COLLECTION OF PHILIP FAHRENHOLZ
Photos on pages 3, 44, 62, 74, and 75

THE COLLECTION OF FRANCES SIEVER
Photos on page 88

THE AUTHOR'S COLLECTION
Photos on pages 5, 18, 36, 50, and 67